RESISTANCE, RESILIENCE, AND RADICAL LOVE

REFLECTIONS ON BLACKNESS AND TEACHING PEACE

REGINA SHANDS STOLTZFUS

Tehom Center Publishing is a 501(c)3 nonprofit publishing feminist and queer authors, with a commitment to elevate BIPOC writers. Its face and voice is Rev. Dr. Angela Yarber.

Paperback ISBN: 978-1-966655-40-4

Ebook ISBN: 978-1-966655-45-9

To my mom, Joyce

Your constant assurance of my capabilities made me believe in myself.

Your love for Black people, Black culture, and Black artistry has gifted me beyond words.

You are, ever and always, my guiding star.

CONTENTS

ACKNOWLEDGMENTS

So much—if not all—of what I know, believe, and strive to live out has been modeled by people in the communities that have shaped me.

I am deeply grateful for my home congregation, Lee Heights Community Church in Cleveland, Ohio. It was there that I first learned how solidarity, justice, grace, and faith intertwine.

I give thanks for the people I've done anti-racism work with over the years—especially the original trainers who helped develop the Damascus Road (now Roots of Justice) training model: Dionicio Acosta, Michelle Armster, Phil Morice Brubaker, Rick Derksen, Calenthia Dowdy, Harley Eagle, Brenda Zook Friesen, Iris de Léon-Hartshorn, Felipe Hinojosa, Erica Littlewolf, Thulani Conrad Moore, Yvonne Platts, Valentina Satvedi Leydon, Tobin Miller Shearer, and Sharon Williams. In so many ways, you helped me find my voice.

I honor the great cloud of witnesses—past, present, and future—names known and unknown, who carry a deep love for and commitment to the Black Freedom Struggle in all its iterations. You have been my teachers. I am in your debt. Thank you for speaking, writing, marching, agitating, loving, and holding fast through even the most treacherous times.

And my students: how you inspire and challenge me. You are living and learning your life's work in a time when the forces of chaos and injustice would love nothing more than to see you give up on your dreams. Please don't. Your brilliance gives me hope.

INTRODUCTION

I have been teaching in higher ed for over fifteen years now, but I didn't plan to be a professor. For a long while, it wasn't clear that I'd even finish college. I had a rough first year and didn't want to go back, so I took a detour from studying to volunteer in a refugee camp in northeast Thailand. It was the late 1970s, and the camp I was assigned to was a temporary home to over 40,000 refugees from Laos, a country the size of Michigan with the distinction of being the most bombed country in the world. Between 1964 and 1973, the U.S. dropped over 2 million tons of cluster bombs on Laos as part of the CIA's attempt to quell communism.

The time between my saying "yes" to the opportunity and moving to Thailand was rushed; I was replacing a volunteer who suddenly couldn't go. It was either a case of right place, right time or pure dumb luck, but within weeks of saying yes, getting a passport and vaccines, and packing some clothes, books, and cassette tapes, I was off. I was nineteen years old and had never been out of the U.S. before. I stepped off the plane in Bangkok for my month-long orientation and my senses were overcome by the heat, the sounds, and the smells. Even the body I lived in felt different—at home I was average height, while in Thailand I felt like I towered over other adults, especially women. A tonal language that I did not speak at all, and an alphabet I could not read were very disorienting. After orientation, which entailed a bit of rudimentary language instruction and introduction to some of the history and culture of Southeast Asia, I was off to the northeast city of Nong Khai, where I would spend most of the next two years. The work was simple enough—helping to prepare and serve food in a supplemental feeding center in the camp—but I was one of the youngest and least experienced of the international workers, and one of very few Black people. I attracted a lot of attention, especially from children. It was intimidating, yet exciting. I lived in town, several kilometers away from the camp. Travel each day was on a tiny automatic motorcycle that made me feel quite cool. I was on the Thai/Cambodian border at a time when thousands walked across the border into the makeshift camp. For those two years I lived among thousands of people who were coping with the traumatic results of long-standing political oppression and war, and that experience impacted the way I understood the world and moved around in it.

My work among refugees was not the first time I was aware of the realities of systemic violence, poverty, and oppression. Those years in Thailand gave me another lens through which to see and understand how structural injustice is supported and perpetuated, and provides benefits to some at the expense (too often deadly) of many. People who believe they stand to gain something – money, status, access –can be convinced to support exploitation and rationalize hierarchies of 'haves' and 'have-nots' kept in their respective positions by normalizing dominance and oppression. It is possible to receive benefits and experience harm in the same body—context matters. In Thailand, my U.S. citizenship stood then, and stands now, in sharp relief against the background of warfare supported by the so-called superpowers. Away from the U.S., my passport afforded me a level of prestige I did nothing to earn, even as my

Blackness was a factor in how people saw and treated me at home and in other countries. In the U.S., our family's race influenced factors such as the neighborhood where my parents could buy a home and the types of jobs they could pursue. The effects of both legal and de facto racial segregation shaped many aspects of life. It was during my parent's young adulthood and my childhood that the Civil Rights Act of 1964 was enacted, despite significant debate and initial weak enforcement. When I was in Thailand, outside of Bangkok, people often associated my black skin with pop culture icons (children might call out "Michael Jackson!" upon seeing me) or with the U.S. military's presence during the Vietnam War period. When I went to Thailand, I was definitely naïve about some things. Initially, I went because I needed something productive to do while taking a break from school. It was a relatively easy adventure to say yes to because I was young and unencumbered by adult responsibilities. I did not know how much the experience would alter the plans I thought I had for my life. When I returned to the U.S., I thought my post-college vocation would be long-term advocacy/service work, ideally with refugees. However, I didn't know exactly what that would look like. Enter college, take two. I lasted another year. Life happened and school went to the back burner again.

In the mid-1990s, I began working with Mennonite Conciliation Service, an agency of Mennonite Central Committee (MCC) U.S., an Anabaptist relief organization. While MCC responded globally to basic human needs like shelter, food, and medical care, MCS's specific mission addressed conflict and advocated for justice. My work included creating and providing mediation and restorative justice resources for individuals and congregations, something I had done on a smaller scale in previous roles with other church agencies. My work gave me the space to think critically about what was for me a curious absence of discussions about race and racism in peacemaking work, at least among the organizations I was most closely connected to (that is, church-related organizations). MCS had a mandate from its inception to include systematic thinking about racism as a peace and justice issue.[1] Taking that mandate seriously, a friend and colleague, Tobin Miller Shearer, and I co-founded an anti-racism education program. At the start, we worked primarily with church organizations within our denomination, the Mennonite Church.[2] With a cohort of trainers and organizers, our network grew to include other denominations such as the United Church of Christ and Episcopal congregations, and secular groups like the National Resource Center on Domestic Violence.

Tobin and I eventually left leadership of this organization, which was then called Damascus Road and now exists under the name Roots of Justice. I went to grad school and got a Ph.D. in theology and ethics. For nearly two decades, I have been teaching peace studies at a small Christian liberal arts college and thinking a lot about what it means to do the work of justice, advocacy, and peacebuilding over the long term, especially when it seems as though the work done by previous generations is unraveling before our eyes. After some serious burnout and the emergence of chronic health issues and witnessing other folks in justice movements also get more and more sick and tired, I wanted—needed—to think more seriously about sustainability. How do we/I keep going? Tobin and I wrote a book about what sustained us in our work and our friendship over 30 years of anti-racism work. So much of liberation work is grounded in the urgency of now, and I can't remember if I ever tried to imagine what the landscape would be like in the decades ahead. And here I am, here we are, living in an era reminiscent of the Reconstruction Era—those years following

---

1. See Michelle Armster. Mennonite Conciliation Service: challenges, successes, and learning. *Intersections: MCC Theory and Practice Quarterly* (blog), September 3, 2020. https://mccintersections.wordpress.com/2020/09/03/mennonite-conciliation-service-challenges-successes-and-learnings/
2. In 2002, the Mennonite Church and the General Conference Mennonite Church merged to become Mennonite Church USA.

the Civil War during which social and political gains for African American were viciously and often violently contested. Seen as an infringement on the Southern way of life, Reconstruction was a threat to white supremacy and the political backlash was intense. Legal challenges and the eventual election of white supremacist leaders eventually dismantled reconstructionist efforts. The struggle continues and I'm staying in it.

But I want to keep doing justice work *and* stay healthy. I want my students to be energized by hope and possibility, even when it seems foolish to do so. And … well, "We who believe in freedom cannot rest" – that is, we cannot quit. I don't believe Ella Baker's iconic words are about not caring for ourselves. It is not a call to work ourselves to death. Instead, her words acknowledge the ongoing necessity of liberation work for the very long haul, with energy that is not grounded in delusion but propelled by visionary hope.

Our knowledge about the human capacity to carry primary and secondary trauma tells us that we have to make choices about how we work around violence and oppression. We don't need more feel-good hero stories that hold up examples of lone individuals who achieved incredible feats because of their extraordinary charisma, courage, and grit. We know those stories are not the whole truth, that change comes about through the concerted efforts of many people working together and caring for each other over the long haul. And we need to know the qualities, conditions, and practices that support long-term social change efforts. We must build the capacity to continue to do the work, because anger and frustration at injustice are not enough to see us through.

Like generations before them, the students I teach are worried about the future. They understandably feel hopeless about the possibility of having a sustainable planet for themselves and the generations after them. I felt this way, too and I know that the communities that held me were part of what made it possible for me to imagine a future for myself in which I not only was able to

thrive but could be an active participant in making things better –
the physical communities of neighborhood, school, and church; the
writers whose books, essays, and poems I read; and my elders, who
did the best they could to teach me my history and call me beloved
in the face of a country that did not see me as such. Those communities informed the way I understand peace and justice work, the
work of liberation.

The impact of the weight of history for African Americans
alongside unrelenting global anti-Blackness and what that ultimately means for the work of peace and justice is sobering. While I
am called and committed to anti-oppression work broadly speaking
and with an intersectional lens, there are points along the way
where I am too tired, too depressed, and too frustrated to want to
keep going. I'm still here, but I am clear that it is not because I am
any more wise or energetic or brilliant than others.

Psychotherapist, activist, and anti-oppression trainer Leticia
Nieto argues that long-term successful social movements go
through several stages: building awareness outside of a small
group of people that something is wrong, documenting the problems, speaking to power holders, doing research, and educating
others. As the movement grows, contagious energy builds and
propels the work. The vision of the issues being resolved also
grows. However, the problem is usually not "solved" because the
powers are invested in keeping the system exactly the way it is
(because it benefits certain people - those with power, with wealth,
those whose identities are valued more than others). Eventually,
the energy and excitement of the movement dissipates. People get
discouraged, they burn out, and may step back or step out because
of fatigue, disappointment, and the seeming impossibility of
change. This can be especially true for those newer at doing movement work. The excitement of demonstrations and protests wears
off. There is likely growing opposition from those invested in the
status quo in the form of labeling activists as subhuman, anti-
American, or whatever words are in vogue for that particular era,

and it all works together brilliantly to wear down a nascent movement. There is a sense of failure and powerlessness, especially since the hits keep coming. For those with "target" identities, there is also the necessity of using survival skills to exist within the reality of ongoing oppression.

But if people in the movement have built capacity and have a wide enough base to sustain energy to keep looking forward, holding up the vision, and employing multiple strategies, it is possible to build a power base which includes pushing back at the power brokers holding the system in place. If they can keep that energy alive, they can push past this stage of heightened hopelessness and burnout.

This, according to Nieto, is where the real work begins. This is where the power brokers declare that the movement has failed while continuing to discredit it. The task of those seeking change is to claim the successes (however small they may seem) and recognize that now is the time to deepen and broaden the movement, involve more people, keep looking ahead, address the opposition that will continue to come, and think systemically. This is the time to honor the importance of the small wins. Educating people, growing the base, and developing a common language are necessary tasks that are less exciting than being among thousands of people at a demonstration, but are essential building blocks. The tipping point comes when society recognizes what activists have done: the talking points, petitions, online education, and continuing organizing work with institutions to foster change beyond the cosmetic. This does not happen quickly.

A semester in a peace studies class demonstrates the arc of this pattern. Students come in with diverse backgrounds and experiences that may have driven their interest in a class focused on peacemaking. Some are already actively engaged in justice movements, on and off campus. Yet even with experience and exposure, a steady diet of thinking, reading, discussing, and writing about violence and injustice over the course of a semester takes a toll—

one I myself was not sufficiently prepared for when I first started teaching. At one semester's end, students in an upper-level class submitted final research papers which were deep dives into specific areas of violence. I read and graded papers about child abuse, sexual assault, genocide, lynching, and more in the short amount of time before my deadline for posting grades. It was a brutal few days of sitting alone with the collective trauma represented in my students' work, instead of being with them and processing as we had done all semester. I didn't know it would be so hard.

But I should have known! At least, this is what I told myself then. Full-time anti-racism work often felt brutal. It was not just the reality of racism past and present, but also the ongoing difficult encounters with people who insisted racism didn't exist in the 20th century, or that the church shouldn't bother itself with such earthly matters, or the many times when my expertise and integrity were questioned. Even with all this, I was under the illusion that if I/we worked hard enough and threw ourselves into the work full tilt (often at the expense of our health, finances, and relationships), we would prevail.

Now, I know better and try to do better. In and out of the classroom, people in liberation movements must create, nurture, and practice strategies that include the whole person. I absolutely include education as liberation movement work. It's a misconception to think that the study of peace (which necessitates the study of violence) is not a kind of justice work, and a further misconception that this work does not affect the spirits and psyches of those engaged in it. It is essential for educators to not only guide the learning process, but to also care for the classroom community as it experiences the heaviness of course material that reflects the context of the actual broken world. The world is overflowing with injustice and oppression, and some of the bodies in the room are experiencing it. We are not removed; we are not separate. Our collective work must fit us for the long haul.

This book is a consideration of that long haul. It's not a movement how-to manual. While there are broad strokes of what liberation work looks like for various issues, and while there are parallels and connections between issues, each time we come to these conversations, context matters. Political landscape, social locations, and cultural zeitgeist shape and reshape the various contexts in which we live and do our work.

The study of violence impacts the psyche; this matters for any person's ability to learn and upon learning, to act. For some educators, it can seem wise to take a clinical, arms-length approach, but the days of pretending that there can be any hint of objectivity about oppression and violence are long gone, at least for me. (This is not to say that an arms-length approach cannot be a good coping tactic—sometimes I need that just to get through the day, like in the aftermath of the killing of Michael Brown in 2014, or the January 6, 2021 insurrection.) Teaching includes multilevel tasks: learning history and theory, using restorative practices on ourselves and with each other, and speaking into systems and structures so that they might become more just. Our bodies, our flesh and blood, our minds need more than 'just the facts.' Just learning the full history and its under- and counter-narratives can produce deep sadness, anger, and guilt that shouldn't be brushed aside. This in turn can ignite a fire to do something besides sit around and study. Students often become impatient about what they may think is useless theory when the world is burning. Others may become hopeless, and others simply check out.

In this book I've tried to gather what I've thought about and learned about myself amidst the seeming futility of so many generations of work for systemic change. While I am dismayed that after years of doing anti-oppression work, the first quarter of the 21st century finds us witnessing the renewed zeal to silence marginalized voices through banning books and censoring the history of the Black people's struggle to exist, much less thrive, in this land mass that became the United States, I am not surprised.

To be sure, my thoughts are not limited to what happens in

peace studies curricula, because these are conversations that extend beyond any one discipline and are all the more critical in an era where such conversations and actions stemming from them are quashed, like the current rollback on Diversity, Equity, and Inclusion (DEI) initiatives by multinational conglomerates and public education systems. This is work that should be incorporated throughout the curriculum. It's not impossible to do. For the past several years, all first-year students at my school read (among other texts) Claudia Rankine's *Citizen: An American Lyric*. A number of the events Rankine writes about happened before these students were born, including Hurricane Katrina and its aftermath and the killing of Trayvon Martin. The book includes an edited version of the iconic photo of a lynching that took place in 1930 in Marion, Indiana – less than two hours' drive from our campus. The original image shows the lynched bodies of Thomas Shipp and Abram Smith, with a crowd of white spectators, gathered around, posing for the camera—some with smiles. Rankine's edited photo only shows the crowd in order to reveal the everyday matter-of-factness of racism and racialized terror of less than a century ago. One man in the crowd looks right at the camera as if he is about to shrug at the mundaneness of it all. Lynchings were public, ritualistic displays of white male power, often justified by claims of protection of white women against Black male predators. (Women and children were also victims of lynching.)

These are histories and perspectives most people educated in the United States do not get, and the impact of learning about them on our present bodies and circumstances is significant, and even more so when they are against the backdrop of the continued suppression of such history. Rankine's magnificent text allows a platform to consider our own experiences and stories, even if those stories never make it into the classroom discussion. Examples from my other classes include introducing students to the 'racial etiquette' of Jim Crow laws and viewing videos on redlining and its continued effects, including the history of the very town we are in as a sundown town.[3] Any discipline can include a conversation about the impact of historical harms like the period of legalized enslavement and genocide of Indigenous people. Including the subject matter is not the problem; it's thinking through how to navigate it as a community. Like our students, many instructors are not accustomed to including this kind of material. Some don't see how it connects with their subject matter or are uncomfortable having any discussions about race. It can be daunting, but that doesn't mean it's not necessary. I have long maintained that one of the reasons we do so poorly at talking about race in this country is because we just don't do it – we don't have the practice at it. Many have been socialized not to, with warnings that it only gets people upset. Some have been raised with the "don't see color" mentality. And there is the notion that these things happened long ago and far away, and it doesn't matter anymore—we're all equal now. All of these sentiments have supported the not so quiet rise of this century's version of white nationalism; people who don't know the past can't imagine the kinds of things that can happen.

Contrary to some propaganda, racism has not ended. While historic gains have been made, our society has again backpedaled with attacks and bans on curricula and resources that would teach accurate history. These dynamics contribute to the fear felt by K-12 educators and college instructors at public schools. Those of us at private liberal arts colleges also have reason to be nervous, especially schools connected to conservative religious organizations that have aligned with Christian nationalism. These tensions come into the classroom with us.

For me, prepping for teaching, grading student work, and keeping current with events means my mind is constantly dwelling upon all the ways human beings can be, have been, and are

---

3. Sundown towns were communities in the U.S. that enforced racial segregation through laws or ordinances, often held in place by violence or the threat of violence. They were called sundown towns because signs warning Black people to make sure to leave before sundown.

currently being horrible to one another. Before my work in higher education, peace education and activism were part of my paid work. As I reflect on so many years of doing this while raising a family and having other responsibilities, I can see the mental, physical, and spiritual toll it took on me and those close to me. It has been costly. Unsurprisingly, many of us also feel guilty for acknowledging this cost, because we know that those who have come before us made it possible for us to be in the places and spaces that we are.

This is all in addition to the typical routines and responsibilities of teaching. In prep, classroom, and assessment, educators consider the arc of the unit, and the place of each unit within the term. We build foundations, introduce concepts and theories, define words. We add layers of complexity to these basic building blocks. We consider and invite, when appropriate, students' lived experiences and how that experience either supports or prevents them from accessing the information, and what needs to be done to bridge gaps. In class we are constantly monitoring the room by observing posture and facial expressions, assessing the energy level in the room, and calculating what we're seeing and feeling to determine if we need to shift directions or make a mental note to check in on someone later. Is a "checked out" student simply tired, hungry, or bored? Or is the student rejecting the information out of hand? Is the student feeling petrified because we're discussing anti-Black racism and they are the only Black student in the class, and petrified that all eyes will turn to them for some supreme wisdom that comes from their experience? Are white and non-Black students of color over it? Is the extra energy involved worth it? Of course it is.

I often tell my students that for me, peace studies and anti-oppression work are more than just academics. I immerse myself in these topics and teach them because the world needs people who think critically, instigate change, care, hold space, and do justice for those hurt by systemic oppression. That is the end game, the reason I keep doing it. It is important to plan ways to keep going, stay healthy, and remain in community with others to sustain my commitment to the work.

Some folks can point to a moment when they became radicalized and joined a movement. Others cannot remember such a moment because they were nurtured in movement work their whole lives and that nurturing has formed their way to be in the world. I think most of us are somewhere along the spectrum between those two poles. Wherever we enter and whatever our lived experience, we all likely know what it is to feel the anger and rage ignited by the ever-present machinery of violence and injustice. Rage is a great energizer. It is appropriate—even necessary—to be angry at injustice. The intense emotional energy of rage is a great mobilizer and pushes many people to participate in the most visible parts of a campaign for change. The energy of anger and frustration drives people to the streets in protest around the globe, with the power to create iconic images that fix movements into our collective memory: the Vietnam War protests, Tiananmen Square, and the Civil Rights Movement, for example. This is what happened after the deaths of Michael Brown in 2014, igniting the Black Lives Matter movement, reigniting with the deaths of George Floyd and Breonna Taylor in 2020. Those who could not take to the streets used the energy generated in other ways to speak out, connect, and draw attention. People were empowered to demand justice because of their overwhelming anger and sadness.

But rage alone doesn't fuel movements for the long haul, and the machinery of oppression will often use our rage to further oppress us, like the stereotype of the Angry Black Woman used to dismiss legitimate rage. Far too often, the rage of marginalized folk, combined with relative powerlessness is turned on ourselves and those who look like us. Rage is a fuel, yes, but it needs to be tempered in the same way metal is to make it durable. First the metal is hardened by subjecting it to a very high temperature, then rapidly cooled. Then it's heated again, this time at a temperature not quite as high as the first time. The first stage makes the metal brittle and prone to easy cracking and breaking. The second stage, the tempering, reduces the brittleness but maintains the toughness, resulting in something far less prone to break under pressure. The process, when done well, is deliberate and careful. Just as overheating tempered steel can damage its structure, unchecked anger can harm relationships, alienate potential allies, and hinder progress.

If rage at injustice is not channeled and managed, it leads to brittle and unsustainable change. Taking to the streets is powerful; it sends a strong message. Protests have power to draw attention and disrupt business as usual, which is vital. But they are only one part of a campaign. Movements need strategic thinking and short- and long-term planning. Flustered power brokers may make some surface level immediate changes due to public outcry, like firing a police officer or sending someone to "diversity training." However, absent a long-range plan, firing or training one person doesn't disrupt unjust, racist structures. The cycle of injustice continues if the root of the problem is not addressed throughout the system. Our quick-fix culture makes imagining such persistence—generational persistence—seem impossible and thankless.

Long-term justice work needs bodies, minds, and spirits that can keep showing up and doing the work. It is not work done with intellect alone. Our bodies, minds, and spirits are affected by injustice. Even when we are not actively engaged in or the receivers of violence done in the name of white supremacy, patriarchy, and other oppressive systems, we are affected by our exposure to them through news reports, social media, and the stories of people around us. Holistic resilience practices for ourselves and our communities are necessary, and we have models of movements that recognize the need to sustain themselves in their struggle.

The Combahee River Collective was established in 1974 by Black women in Boston and named for the Combahee River in South Carolina, where Harriet Tubman liberated more than 750 enslaved people. The 1977 Collective statement expressed a full-hearted commitment to combating racial, sexual, heterosexual, and class oppression. It emphasized the need for an integrated analysis recognizing the interconnected nature of major oppressive systems. The synthesis of these oppressions, they argued, forms the backdrop of Black women's lives, positioning what they named Black feminism as the logical political movement to confront the simultaneous oppressions faced by all women of color. The collective, including founding members Barbara Smith and Beverly Smith, laid the groundwork for the Combahee River Collective Statement, a foundational text in Black feminist theory. The statement underscored the importance of centering marginalized voices within the feminist and civil rights movements, with a focus on economic justice. The energy with which they describe their finding one another, the naming of their realities, and the power of sharing stories, crafting an intersectional analysis, and building a community around the analysis reminds me of the same energy and power I experienced when working in collective spaces.

The Combahee statement argues that "the only people who care enough about us to work consistently for our liberation are us."[4] This assertion flies in the face of notions of voicelessness, a term unfortunately bandied about by supposed allies and activists, even in the 21st century. No one is voiceless. Let's be honest: the 'voiceless' are people who are not listened to, not seen, people who are ignored, discounted and pushed away because of their identities.

Those with more social power can use their power to speak to and dismantle systems of oppression. They must also work with their own people and follow the leadership of marginalized folk. They must understand that Black people and other people of color

---

4. Combahee River Collective. "The Combahee River Collective Statement," Home Girls: A Black Feminist Anthology, Barbara Smith, editor. New York: Kitchen Table-Women of Color Press, 1983, 275.

know best what white supremacy and its bedfellows are doing to us. This too often has not been the case. When so-called allies are more interested in policing tone and tactics than dismantling systems of oppression, it's easy to see why "giving voice to the voiceless" is such an attractive motivation. It's easier to speak over and for the people society has already worked hard to silence. It's more complicated to work out how to be in solidarity, to be in community and conversation (speaking and listening) with oppressed people. Insisting that dissent be polite, or withdrawing support for a movement because one doesn't understand and/or agree with tactics, says clearly that actual, substantial change is not really desired. These kinds of divisions are supported by white supremacy and patriarchy. Those systems rely upon a hierarchy that perpetuates an 'us/them' dynamic even in our movements.

The Black Panther Party was another movement that tightly connected Black oppression to capitalism and sought to address physical, economic, and psychological violence against Black people. The Party's "Survival Programs" of the 1960s provided essential resources to Black communities, including free breakfasts for children, community learning centers, and organized Black Student Alliances to challenge racism in schools. The Black Panther Party insisted on teaching accurate Black history and the power of political activism, while the mainstream politics of the time were insisting Black poverty and struggle were directly connected to Black culture and dysfunctional Black family systems. Today, the same arguments are being made.

Both the Combahee River Collective and the Black Panther Party were movements of their times that existed because people recognized the need to put their own hands and intellect into the work of liberation and build sustainable systems of doing that work. This history inspires me to continue showing up for my community, children, ancestors, and myself.

It can be easy to look at the "big" accomplishments of movements and miss how they are undergirded by a foundation of tending to the physical, emotional, and spiritual health of the collective, especially when these histories are suppressed. Individualistic societies downplay the importance of holding a communal story and understanding the importance of smaller acts—the day-to-day workings and daily practices of peacemaking work, like sharing stories and food, empathy, and kindness. Without a foundation, structures easily crumble. A recent incident reminded me of this.

It was late in the semester with maybe a month or so to go. I had just finished teaching a night class. This is the part of the semester where everyone is tired, stressed, and maybe a little cranky because the finish line is still weeks away. Before shutting off my "work brain" for the night, I glanced at email on my phone. A high-ranking administrator at my college had written to me to ask about the progress of a project I was working on in collaboration with several people from other institutions. The early stages of the project had hit a lot of snags, and we were behind schedule. I sighed as I skimmed the email. Rather than heading into a restful evening, I began to shame spiral for my part in the delays. Then I started to get annoyed and angry because clearly, this administrator did not understand how much I had on my plate. I resisted the temptation to open my computer and reread the email. Instead, I started composing an angry and self-righteous reply in my head, ticking off all of the things I *had* been accomplishing over the semester.

The following day, I reread the administrator's email. I was wrong. The tone I thought was there the night before (when I was tired, hungry, and just done teaching a 2 1/2-hour class) was not there. The administrator had asked where we were on the project and what we needed to see it through to completion. Instead of a dressing-down, it was a calling in—into account for something I was responsible for—and more importantly, an expression of care and an offer of assistance.

Feeling better and somewhat chastened, I went to the rest of my email. There was one from a student asking to meet so that we could fix a scheduling problem "as soon as possible." I had previously contacted this student a number of times with no success to avoid this very issue. Now the student had an emergency of their own making: because they had not registered in time they were now waitlisted for a required class that would not come around again for a year. Annoyed, I again started writing an email in my head, scolding the student for not doing what they should've done earlier and saying that I would not be able to meet with them because I had other things going on. Then I realized I was doing the exact thing I thought had been done to me. I didn't know the whole story—why the student missed appointments, and why they didn't respond to my emails. When I replied, I wrote what I hoped was kind instead of the passive aggressive retort I initially wanted to send. I said we could probably do some thinking with each other over email, but I wouldn't be able to meet right away, and I added that I was sorry that they got closed out of the class, but we'd figure something out. To be completely honest, I was still slightly annoyed, because part of college is learning to manage one's life and schedule. But so is having a job. That day, I was reminded of how I can be perceived, how I perceive others, what that means for our relationships, and the options I have for problem-solving that align with my ethics. This is true in work and school and especially in our organizing for change!

I want to be treated fairly and with kindness, even if someone is annoyed with me or just having a bad day. I want to treat others with kindness as a default, even when I'm stressed. I want to be the kind of professor and mentor that holds students (and myself) to high standards but leaves room for all of us to be human— because we are, and we will miss the mark. From this starting point, we build a foundation for justice work, make it possible to have authentic conversations about complex subjects, and prepare ourselves to create the world we envision.

In large part, this book is an account of my thoughts and

attempts to not give in to despair while teaching about violence and oppression. I write from the location of my embodiment and experience—that of a Black woman living in the United States and doing much of her work in the context of predominantly white institutions in various stages of doing their work. I write because I have been held and nurtured by communities that have helped me survive. There have also been communities that have failed me and people who look like me. This book is for anyone who resonates with my experiences and my questions. Others are welcome to listen in and take what is useful.

I frame my peacemaking educating through an anti-racism lens, and the lens of my experience and understanding of anti-Blackness in the United States and across the globe. Working in this framework does not mean that I don't know and understand how other groups are affected by racism. I am assuredly in solidarity with everyone affected by white supremacy and colonialism (and the other isms). Yet, I also must center the particular racialized history in the United States born and perpetuated by the theft and enslavement of millions of Africans and their descendants. That history exists alongside the specific racialized history of this land's indigenous people. Having a deep understanding of anti-Blackness and how it has functioned historically and continues to do so in the present is essential for facing how racism functions in the U.S. context, and this focused understanding has much to teach us about the insidious nature of systemic oppression and how it reshapes and perpetuates itself to fit any era and any circumstance. Anti-Blackness has always sought to convince poor white people, other people of color, and Black people ourselves to disparage, discount, and seek to destroy Black people and our culture. I cannot authentically engage in peace and justice studies without this lens.

In Derrick Bell's *Faces At the Bottom of the Well: The Permanence of Racism*, the author notes how politicians scapegoat Black people for failed economic or political policies: "Before the Civil War, rich slave owners persuaded the white working class to stand with them against the danger of slave revolts—even though the existence of slavery condemned white workers to a life of economic privation. After the Civil War, poor whites fought social reforms and settled for segregation rather than see formerly enslaved blacks get ahead."[5] Bell noted that the same tactics in the pre-and post-Civil War era also worked in the 1980s and 90s. And they continue to work in the 21st century.

I have lived long enough now to see first-hand the repercussions and backlashes waged against any hint of Black progress or even Black well-being. They show up as a consistent barrage of microaggressions in the convenient and anonymous town square provided by the internet: why isn't there a white history month (yes, people still ask that), complaints about diversity initiatives and hiring/admission policies... And they show up in policies and legislation meant to erode any gains that might disrupt white comfort—the banning of teaching books and the teaching of history, the rollback of affirmative action programs, and the dismantling of DEI offices. As Bell says, "...the code words differ. (but) The message is the same."

As you read, I invite you to reflect on your own journey, social location, and lens. If you are Black, how has your lived experience shaped your understanding of systemic racism and your approach to justice work? What have you learned from the generations before you, and what are you learning from young people?

For non-Black people of color, what intersections do you see between anti-Black racism and the forms of oppression that have touched your life and community? And for white people, what story do you bring to engaging with these issues, and how do your

---

5. Bell, Derrick. *Faces At the Bottom of the Well: The Permanence of Racism.* New York, NY: Basic Books, 1992. https://hdl-handle-net.ezproxy.goshen.edu/2027/heb33001. 0001.001. PDF.

own experiences and position in society inform your commitment to this work?

These questions are not merely academic; they form a foundation of how we can show up in anti-oppression spaces and how we keep this critical work moving forward, especially now when the stakes seem even higher. As you read, please keep returning to your own story, examining how it shapes your perspective and practice. Understanding our different starting points and lived experiences invites opportunities to acknowledge the unique wisdom and challenges we each bring to the work of building a more just world.

1

TEACHING PEACE MEANS STUDYING VIOLENCE

ONE DAY, I WALKED INTO MY CLASSROOM EXPECTING the usual pre-class chatter from my students as they settled in. Instead, I overheard the tail end of a pretty somber discussion as they shared reading strategies for the book we were reading—a memoir of a person's recovery after having been brutally raped and left for dead by the rapist. The students advised each other not to read the book before going to sleep, not to read alone in the room, and so on—almost like tips on watching a horror film. In this case, the horror we were reading was real. This class is called Personal Violence and Healing, an upper-level course in which we spend the first half of the semester learning about cycles of violence and the associated traumas that accompany these cycles. Accounts of rape, genocide, war, and other atrocities are our weekly fare. Many of the classes I teach are variations on these themes, so I am living with this content in one way or another—as part of my job and living in a violence-prone world—most of the time.

The conversation was not surprising, and I was proud of them for developing and sharing coping strategies. I remember clearly the first time a student broke down during a reading discussion in this class in an earlier year. The student admitted to not completing the reading assignment but still had something they wanted to say. They noted that the author's description of a brutal sexual assault was too close to home – they had experienced this as well. The more the student talked, the more their voice broke until there was nothing but tears. The rest of the room was silent. This was the same semester a student (not in this class, and not one I had known) had been the victim of a murder/suicide less than two miles from our campus.

In a different class, during an earlier year, a male student leapt to has feet in the middle of class to loudly express his frustration over the amount of time our class was discussing men's violence against women. While we named and discussed violence against all genders, overwhelming statistics show most violence against women and girls is perpetrated by men. This student complained "not all men," and that he, himself, was not a rapist or an abuser of women and girls. He demanded more time be given to discussion about women's violence against men and boys.

In the heat of moments like these—what to do? When class is disrupted for any reason, an immediate response is necessary. In these cases (and for me there have been a number of them) responses include caring for students in distress, holding space for other stories told and untold in the room, and considering how these incidents could impact the rest of the course. The person in charge has to make whatever happens fit the amount of time available in the session, so it matters if it's the beginning, middle, or end of class. Do you let the event take over the rest of the session? Is everyone safe? How will we (or will we) acknowledge this moment going forward when this unit is done and we move to the next one? The two examples are on the milder end of the spectrum of possibilities. There have been at least three times during my teaching career when a man bigger than me exploded in anger at our course content. I felt unsafe in those moments, but I was still responsible for the people in the room.

In both of these examples, each of the students were expressing needs. They were responding to our course content in the light of their lived experiences (and their interpretations of those experiences) in ways that educators hope happens for students. However, these and other reactions are not just individual perspectives. These perspectives exist within and are shaped by social identities and the larger social/political/historical context. Educators must discern on the fly what kind of caretaking is necessary and appropriate in these moments. The second student's anger and frustration mirror the reactions I and other anti-oppression educators get when teaching/talking about systems of oppression and their effects. Because a primary focus of my work is race, and because I have mostly worked in predominantly white settings, I have often received pushback (ranging from "gentle" to outright hostile) when naming racism as a systemic, deeply embedded reality that has real effects on real people up to the present moment. Others who do this work will recognize these dynamics, but it doesn't have to be a part of one's work – go on any social media site where race is introduced as a factor and watch the inevitable pushback. These situations don't happen every day, but the awareness of these potential dynamics is necessary as we plan, navigate the semester, and reflect on what we've done when the semester is over. Even if someone does not break down in tears or have a frustrated outburst, I am consistently aware that we are at various places of knowing and being in the world as a class community, and that matters for what is possible each session, each semester.

In a perfect world, everyone would know what they are getting into when enrolling in these classes. My students see pain and suffering caused by violence, and many of them have experienced it directly. They want to change the world. They are passionate and are full of energy. But when we get into the thick of three months of processing the reality of how this violence lands on bodies and psyches, the energetic spark is dimmed for many of them. It's not that they no longer care—it is the overwhelming feeling of knowing too much about how much horror is out there and how long it has been in place. I too am affected by this knowledge. Even with my many more years of thinking about conflict and violence, I still needed to develop new strategies for my psychological, physical, and spiritual health to keep teaching this content and live in the world as it is.

Violence does not stop, and peace does not happen because we talk about it and study it. So some would call the study futile. But we must study it—peace education and justice work demand a deep understanding of how violence and oppression function, and of the narratives that people, especially those positioned at the top of social hierarchies, are socialized into. Their socialization is necessary to keep the machinery of oppression well oiled, functioning, and able to adjust to the times. If we want justice brought by systemic change, we need that deep understanding and the ability to discuss it with each other and those who oppose us. We need the capacity to hold complexity and the resources to do inner and community-based work.

What we do to create a more just world requires a deep well of inner resources, strength, and conviction. For those of us who face ongoing oppression and the denial of our humanity because of our identities, the need for resilience, resistance, and radical love is paramount. Author and activist adrienne maree brown writes, "Things are not getting worse, they are getting uncovered. We must hold each other tight and continue to pull back the veil."[1]

This is especially true for those who are called to do anti-oppression work in isolated settings because of where we work and live, like academics who teach from a social justice perspective in predominantly white institutions and folks who work with or within predominantly white religious organizations. These are the

---

1. Adrienne Maree Brown. Living Through the Unveiling (blog). Adrienne Maree Brown, February 3 2017, https://adriennemareebrown.net/2017/02/03/living-through-the-unveiling/

contexts in which I have worked most often, and I have seen many colleagues leave these spaces for the good of their mental, physical, and spiritual health. For now, I have chosen to stay. The work is necessary, fulfilling, and it brings me joy, but it is hard.

I came to higher ed from a background of teaching conflict transformation and mediation in workshop settings with adults. While the goals are the same in each setting, modification for each audience is needed. In one setting, the one my work was formed in, I worked mostly with adults who had chosen to be in the work-shop. In the classroom I'm mostly with 18- to 22-year-olds with a wide variety of reasons to be in a particular class: interest, curios-ity, passion... or the time of the course just fits their schedule, and they need the credit.

The pressure of time and getting through content is funda-mental in the classroom and workshops because time is limited and at some point we have to end. In a workshop, though, one does not have the pressure of grades, which allows more flexibility with how content is presented and time spent in each session. In each setting, voices and stories are essential for building commu-nity and learning to speak across boundaries. So, we tell stories. We listen to each other. In one class, an assignment that allows (ok, requires) students to share a bit of what brings them joy and hope or to talk about where they see resilience and strength allows us to begin each session with a transition that says, "We are here to do the work of peacebuilding, and here is a story to ground us." In a culture that values efficiency and speed, taking the time to tell stories may seem like needless fluff to many whose attitude toward learning might be more like, "Just give me the info, let me repeat it back to you, and we'll call it done."

While there is a real temptation to be efficient by cutting out portions of the class that don't seem "academic" or are pedagogi-cally different from what students have experienced in other settings, I know taking the time to be explicit at the beginning of the semester about the importance of creating community is worth it. And I have learned to trust more and more that sticking with community care practices throughout the semester is even more valuable. Being a community means that it's more likely that we can develop strategies to help us move through the inevitable painful material. Some folks think this is a waste of time and that doing so feeds into the notion that "kids today are just too fragile." This is an unfair accusation and feeds into a tired resignation that because the world is brutal, we all need to toughen up. This is not too far from platitudes like "might makes right" and the idea that to succeed one must put on a tough façade and knock everyone else out of the way in order to survive in the classroom and life. These kinds of arguments appeared when educators began the practice of giving content warnings for some material. Similar accusations about "snowflakes" within social justice warrior ranks (also a slur against progressive-leaning folks) were and are part of an orchestrated backlash against people who understood the effects of trauma and secondary trauma and are part of a more extensive campaign to shut down exactly the kind of education I do. I don't want my classrooms to become more humane and trauma-informed because my students are fragile; I want it because I want them to have the capacity to work for justice for the long haul. At this very writing, books are being banned, DEI efforts are being dismantled and erased, and entire fields of study are under fire due to "anti-woke" legislation. I want to help us *all* develop practices to build and sustain that capacity and realize the long and beautiful legacy of resistance strategies we must build upon. We don't have to reinvent the wheel, but we do need to reshape it for our particular circumstances, including the powers' resistance to resistance. We are not only working against the effects of systemic violence but also the forces that keep it in place because it benefits them.

In 1960, Black college students at Fisk University led an intense, multi-week campaign to desegregate downtown Nashville lunch counters. They had been inspired by college students in

Greensboro, North Carolina, who had led a similar campaign earlier in the year. The Greensboro students had studied non-violent protest independently and meticulously planned a sit-in. The next day, other students joined the protest, and by the end of the week, students from different colleges (including some white students) took part. The protests expanded to other stores and other lunch counters, even as they faced harassment by crowds of angry white people. But the numbers of the lunch counter protesters grew, and by the next week, college students throughout the south were staging protests of their own.

Many of today's college students, especially if they were educated in predominantly white schools, only have a dim aware-ness of the Civil Rights Movement, especially events that were not dominated by the "big names" of the movement. They know the big names (even if they know them in a mythologized way). They don't know as well the crucial roles played by people their age who were much of the power behind strategies that led to the end of legalized race-based segregation. The Nashville students attended training sessions and practiced non-resistance tactics led by their elders in the movement. On the surface, the strategy seemed simple: go to the lunch counter, quietly take a seat, and refuse to leave when told they wouldn't be served. Each day, the Black students came and sat. In response to their tactics, some lunch counters shut down and didn't serve anyone. Some white customers stopped having lunch in the stores. The campaign disrupted business as usual in the stores and the city. Students were arrested, which was part of the plan to call attention to what was happening in Nashville and other cities. Despite the escalating harassment and outright violence by white citizens and law enforcement, the students persisted, returning week after week. The resolution did not appear as quickly as it had in Greensboro, but the energy of the movement across the south was palpable.

Violence against the students and others who joined the protest accelerated. The home of Z. Alexander Looby, the lawyer representing students who were arrested, was bombed. But instead of quieting down and going away, they kept going, and more people joined the campaign. The day Looby's house was bombed, thousands of Nashville residents marched to city hall. Black people from all over the city put their bodies on the line by joining the campaign. Black clergy asked Mayor Ben West to come out and talk to the crowd. On the steps of city hall, college student Diane Nash (85 years old at the time of this writing) pointedly asked the mayor, "Do you feel it is wrong to discriminate against a person solely on the basis of their race or color?" Caught in the gaze of thousands of Nashville residents and the press recording the moment, West agreed it was wrong. Three weeks later, the lunch counters were open to serve Black people. The sit-ins had lasted four months, from February to May. Nash became a founding member of the Student Nonviolent Coordinating Committee and would go on to be a Freedom Rider, protesting segregated bus transportation across the South.

The lunch counter protests were strategic, in-your-face actions, the kind taken by local folks worldwide to bring attention to injustice and force systemic change. They were not and are not the only tactics a long-range campaign uses; like other strategies, they have a specific role in the overall campaign. But this kind of visibility and tenacity was critical in racial desegregation nationwide. This multigenerational campaign and others, like the Freedom Rides, are reminders that change is possible even in the face of violent opposition. Some of us will see the changes we are working for in our lifetimes, and many of us will not. Importantly, they are reminders that everyday people make change happen.

Long-term/lifetime commitment to a cause is sustained when the people involved are themselves sustained. The students in Nashville disrupted their lives for four months. They met opposition but were supported in many ways by each other and the communities surrounding them. For many of them, it was local clergy and other church folks.

Such support also matters for the study of violence and movements to end violence. A semester's worth of study is stressful not only because of the subject matter but because we are doing this while also living in the world we are learning about. We are existing with the hardships of the present moment, compounded by the modern reality that we can know all the harm happening around the world in an instant. We were not created to withstand such knowledge, but here we are. Our histories can be good teachers to help prepare us.

Histories of liberation movements are testimonies to endurance. Those who are not facing the same oppressions in the same ways as past generations may think we have no right to need coping strategies. Many of us were taught that the hardships and sacrifices made by our ancestors are the reason we are here and that we dishonor their memories by not grinding as hard as we can for as long as we can, no matter the cost. It is true that each generation owes something to those who paved the way, and also to the descendants that will follow. But we often do not sufficiently also honor how our forebears took care of their communities and themselves and crafted hard-won space for joy and celebration. Many liberation movements have built life-giving strategies into their community life and work. We have more information about the struggles fought because that is what has been captured and recorded as official records of movements. Even so, amid struggle, the artists were creating, the singers were singing, the healers were healing, and the teachers were teaching. The work of each generation keeps us going by bearing witness to the past, honoring the work done by those before us, grieving the losses and celebrating the gains, and doing our part for our time. This is my philosophy of teaching about violence.

During my years of doing anti-racism education and organizing, the work was hard, joyful, frustrating, and rewarding—often all at once. While I didn't think that our work would end racism and all other human-facilitated oppressions forever, I naively did not foresee some thirty years later that structural racism would continue to be so deeply entrenched and that there would be a resurgence of emboldened white supremacist thought and action not only in the public square but in local and national legislative bodies as well. The times swing back and forth like a pendulum. The gains of the Civil Rights Movement and other liberation movements swung the pendulum toward hope. It's not surprising that "hope" was a central theme of the Obama campaign, and it's also not a surprise that there are those who are hellbent on making this country's marginalized bodies pay for two terms of a Black family occupying the White House. Despite the gains of generations past, persistent inequality and deeply rooted injustices persist, and anti-Black racism still runs deep in the veins of this land birthed by colonization and enslavement. Despite the scores of folks who have worked against systems of oppression, those systems remain firmly entrenched. It is difficult not to despair.

In the summer of 2020, the names of Ahmaud Arbery, Breonna Taylor, and George Floyd joined the litany of names of unarmed Black people killed at the hands of law enforcement. During that pandemic summer, massive protests erupted in cities around the world and many people said they were educating themselves by starting/joining book clubs and online discussion groups. There was also the growing energy of those who pushed back at any of the gains made regarding race in the 21st century, initiating a sea of legislation explicitly addressing education: who gets to tell what stories and how. At the heart of many of these bills is the sentiment that white people should not have to feel uncomfortable about any of the history that has created what we as a nation experience today. We have seen this before.

Backlash aside, an additional overwhelming factor in the classroom is that this history is complex, multilayered, and centuries-long. As an educator trying to make it make sense to people who have no context for this information or have a particular and personal context, I find it helpful to start with three simple questions around which to frame content: what happened (event), why did it happen (historical context), and what do we do now (how do we change it/keep it from happening again)?

The third question is my motivation for teaching, speaking, and writing. They are my "why." There are times when I am much more prone to pessimism and wanting to check out than I was years ago. It's not that my "all in" posture of years past was better. There were several unhealthy patterns: overwork, not tending to my health, and not tending to my relationships in ways that could and should have sustained me, my family, and my community. It's easy to get caught up in the trap of thinking my/our activism is nothing if it is not everything. This is a problem exacerbated by the exhaustion brought on once society entered the 24-hour news cycle era and now the ability to be digitally connected to so much information all the time. Instead of all of this access being freeing, it can be paralyzing. We put pressure on ourselves and each other to "get it right"—use the right words, fight for the right causes, and play into the Oppression Olympics. We burn ourselves out and are in constant danger of eating our own, losing sight of the real enemy. I think the power of art is part of the remedy.

Artist Kara Walker grew up watching her father make art, and decided she wanted to do the same. A MacArthur genius grant recipient at the age of 27, Walker paints, draws, produces films, and sculpts. She is perhaps best known for her cut-out paper silhouettes of people and scenes, many of which address the macabre history of U.S. slavery and racial violence. Walker's likely most controversial work was a gigantic, temporary sculpture made of sugar: a sphinxlike woman created to commemorate the demolition of the Domino Sugar factory in Brooklyn, NY. Walker's full title of the massive work was the following:

At the behest of Creative Time
Kara E. Walker has confected:

A Subtlety

or the *Marvelous Sugar Baby*

an Homage to the unpaid and overworked Artisans who
have refined our Sweet tastes from the cane fields to the
Kitchens of the New World
on the Occasion of the demolition of the Domino Sugar
Refining Plant

The pure white sculpture portrayed a bare-breasted woman with a
kerchief on her head. It was a massive rendering of a sugar subtlety
—a sweet fondant dessert molded as a figure to serve medieval
kings. The sculpture marked the centuries of human trafficking
that traded sugar for bodies and bodies for sugar.

According to the curator's statement:

> ... Walker's sphinx is a hybrid of two distinct racist stereo-
> types of the black female: She has the head of a kerchief-
> wearing black female, referencing the mythic caretaker of
> the domestic needs of white families, especially the raising
> and care of their children, but her body is a veritable carica-
> ture of the overly sexualized black woman, with prominent
> breasts, enormous buttocks, and protruding vulva that is
> quite visible from the back. If this evocation of both care-
> giver and sex object—complicated by her coating in white
> sugar—feels offensive, it is meant to. It is part of what
> Walker has come to be known for.

The piece was a commentary on race, gender, class, economics,
poverty, wealth, and empire. An artistic rendering, yes. A conversa-

tion starter. But it was also an in-your-face reckoning with history. It was an answer to the questions:

- What happened?
- Why did it happen?
- What do we do now?

These questions keep the history we must know in order to do the work of our era in front of us. Artists of many mediums help tell the stories, acknowledging the reality of individual and collective trauma and developing language to continue to do so.

A sculpture also commemorates the Nashville sit-ins. Dedicated in 2017, "Witness Walls" in Nashville is a memorial created by a collection of broken concrete walls that bear the images of people who participated in the decades-earlier movement.

Activists and others involved in anti-oppression work must work to craft, tend to, and defend protected spaces for themselves and their communities. The term "safe space" has been criticized, and alternatives such as "safer space" have been proposed. However, the term "protected space" may be the most helpful in describing the type of space activists and individuals engaged in anti-oppression work need. Even so, access to art and art education is diminishing for students in underserved public schools— deemed luxuries rather than necessities. Yet artists are the interpreters of the times and culture. Expressing joy and pain through movement, play, and art is essential for human development, mental health, and liberation.

Social change comes about because of many factors, including collective action. Equally important is the creation of protected spaces for marginalized communities. Marginalized and oppressed folk have always worked together to create spaces where we can support each other and work towards a common goal. Such work is the foundation of a sustained commitment to self-care and community care.

Self-care and community care are not one size fits all—we enter the work of liberation in different ways, which ebb and flow depending upon our circumstances and stage of life. For three decades, my primary involvement has been teaching, being in conversation about structural and systemic issues, and working at getting folks to see where they fit in—as targets and survivors of particular kinds of structural violence or as those on whose behalf the violence is done. This knowledge is crucial in an age of accusations demonizing critical race theory and the accurate teaching of history.

The 2020 pandemic was deeply polarizing for a country already riven by a contentious presidential election and deepening political divides. These divides became more deeply entrenched as rancorous debates about masks, vaccines, and critical race theory accompanied the health care crisis coupled with social isolation. Where I live, In a predominantly white town in a red state, daring to run a minor errand with a mask on my Black face felt frankly dangerous. Each time I left my home, I felt anxious about my safety. This ramped up the challenges I felt about teaching my subject matter. My colleagues and my students were also dealing with these challenges, while trying to do school online like millions of other people. On any given day, my brain would be ping-ponging between thoughts of "this is what we need to talk about now while the world is on fire!" and "How can I keep thinking about all of this and require my students to think about it with me?" Opting out was not an option. Even so, it would have been wrong to press on as if our course content was unrelated to events outside the classroom, including the pandemic and its effects.

Further, my classes focus on violence and conflict, all of the isms: racism, sexism, classism, ableism, heterosexism, colonialism, and more. In large part, an intersectional analysis necessitates holding the web of oppressions and their effects together in as complete a cloth as we can create. It would not do the work justice to pretend these oppressions are not intricately woven together, creating a fabric that covers us all and affects us in different ways but spells disaster for our shared future. Students, faculty, and staff —heck, all of society—needed support. The level of crisis I heard about in just one week overwhelmed me—one student's attempted suicide, panic attacks in the classroom, families dealing with loss of work, illness, and death. So, things began to change. In the midst of all this, it was time to revise my teaching—again.

My earlier context of anti-oppression work was facilitating workshops with participants spending several days together, usually a weekend plus some travel time. Time was short, and we had to get it all in! Working primarily with employed adults who had opted in meant that our training teams didn't have to think as much about human developmental stages. When I shifted to the college classroom, at first, I mistakenly brought this same energy. My zeal to get it all out there was stressful to everyone. It wasn't that the students needed different information; instead, I needed to adapt to the context—primarily traditionally college-age students. They were not less intelligent; they were not absent of lived experience; they just had less of it, and other things going on in their brains. It was unfair of me to bypass that reality and expect something different. Perhaps most college professors come equipped with that knowledge and expertise learned from their programs; I came into higher ed as a second career educator before completing my Ph.D.

I learn something of student's stories through class discussions and reflection papers. Often their self-disclosures reveal the ways in which they experience violence—our subject matter. I tell my students early and often that they are never required to share anything they don't want to in discussion or reflection papers, and I don't ask for their harrowing stories. Spoken or not, the stories are present because they resonate with the course materials and with current events. Their/our stories of hurt and trauma can and do enter the conversation. We don't have to rely on outside resources to learn, for instance, about the harms of anti-immigrant sentiments and the results of over-surveilled communities and underfunded schools, because so many of us have firsthand, experiential knowledge—we are living it. I would not survive teaching for the long haul unless I got serious about building more structure for self-care and mutual support, for my own sake and theirs.

Committing to societal healing means paying attention to the wounds we carry as individuals and making the same commitment to healing ourselves as individuals. This is vital for those of us who have been conditioned to be the nurturers instead of the nurtured. Black women have an entire set of stereotypes built around being simultaneously strong and capable of bearing any burden, yet also incompetent and not to be trusted. These stereotypes are not just annoying; they are an extension of violence. Historical and contemporary examples abound, including Tressie McMillan Cottom's recounting in her book *Thick: And Other Essays* how a series of medical professionals ignored, talked over, and neglected her needs as she went into pre-term labor with a daughter who died shortly after birth. Cottom sat bleeding in an emergency waiting room for hours. She was sent home by a doctor who told her that her weight was likely the cause of the spotting. After enduring three days of pain, she went back to the hospital, where an ultrasound showed a baby and two tumors. Cottom was then admonished for not saying she was in labor and subsequently treated unkindly by several other healthcare professionals.

> When we perform some existential service to men, to capital, to political power, to white women, and even to other 'people of color' who are marginally closer to white than they are to black, then we are superwomen. We are fulfilling our purpose in the natural order of things. When instead black women are strong in service to ourselves, that same

strength, wisdom, and wit become evidence of our incompetence.[2]

Far too many stories like this demonstrate the lack of empathy for Black bodies that leads to the suffering those same Black bodies are ultimately blamed for. So much more than "self-care" is needed to withstand this reality. The term self-care has become commodified and reduced to meaning gratuitous pampering and feeding into the numbing effects of consumerism. Audre Lorde's claim "Caring for myself is not self-indulgence, it is self-preservation, and that is an act of political warfare" is a critical truth. Self-preservation is the foundation of the ability to do justice work for the sake of my people, my community, and, ultimately, the world. If we do not believe deep in our bones that we are worth being whole and healthy, we lose the capacity to do our work well and sustainably. This doesn't mean things are not worth doing if our personal care goals are unmet. It does mean actively resisting messages that say our lives are not worth saving. This is the way structural violence and injustice begin—with the assertion and normalization of dehumanization. The rhetoric of war predictably relies upon constructing an enemy that poses a threat, and therefore, that enemy must not only be stopped but vanquished. The justification for upholding legalized enslavement based on race and later, the enforcement of segregation, employed the same logic. Individual and collective self-preservation's first steps are recognizing those patterns and interrupting them when others do it, and when we do it to ourselves or people who look like us. We must understand that self-hatred is often a trauma response.

Trauma overwhelms a person's ability to cope and leaves them feeling helpless; it creates a person's experience of the world as an unsafe, unpredictable place. Traumatic events that are repeated and

---

2. Cottom, Tressie McMillan, "Dying to Be Competent" in Thick: And Other Essays, The New Press, 2019, pg. 93.

prolonged, like sexual abuse, domestic violence, bullying, and the systemic violence of poverty, racism, sexism, and more, lead to complex or chronic trauma. While reading about another person's complex trauma, my students instinctively developed strategies for helping each other process trauma, that of others and their own. For some of them, the course content activated responses to their own trauma.

When we read and discuss accounts of rape, lynching, and ongoing abuses by systems we have been told are good and trustworthy, emotional, spiritual, and physiological responses are expected. For some, this knowledge is a profound reordering of a worldview that creates significant cognitive dissonance. For them, the world so far had been safe. Others feel relief because their knowledge of the world as unsafe is recognized and affirmed in the classroom, perhaps for the first time. This relief may also help process the feelings of rage, grief, and despair such knowledge brings.

Racialized trauma results from direct racist harassment or attacks, witnessing racist police brutality or race-based violence (in person or via social media), relentless microaggressions, and the ongoing effects of systemic, institutionalized racism that is historical, intergenerational, and contemporary. While learning about it, it's simultaneously happening. The past is not past, and our bodies respond in the way that they are programmed. When faced with danger, a complex system of physiological changes kicks in, because our bodies are wise and work to keep us safe and alive. The stress hormones cortisol and adrenaline are released, increasing heart rate, blood pressure, and blood sugar levels to prepare the body to protect itself or flee. We breathe more deeply to take in more oxygen, and our blood vessels direct blood flow to our muscles, heart, and lungs to maximize the ability to confront or escape. That "fight-or-flight response" functions to keep us alive, but cumulative stress responses are not a good thing; they lead to hypervigilance, anxiety, depression, and susceptibility to chronic physical health conditions. The flow of excess cortisol affects sleep and appetite. Constant fight-or-flight response cycles wreak havoc on the body with aches and pains. The immune system is weakened and less able to fight infection. Extended periods of elevated cortisol are linked to higher rates of hypertension, heart disease, diabetes, cancer, and early cognitive decline or dementia. Spiritual health is affected as trauma can shatter beliefs about divine goodness, protection, or justice.

Educators need to be aware of the effects of this on students, themselves, and the people in their lives. Individual and collective healing from racist trauma requires not only tending to individual but also societal efforts toward justice; this includes repairing past and ongoing harms, even as these kinds of efforts are regularly under attack. The pushback on K -12 curricula, public university recruiting, and programming has historical precedence. Campaigns against "wokeism" diminish the kind of support needed by all students to help them understand and thrive in a complex and hurting world, and be equipped to bring about change.

My parents migrated to Cleveland, Ohio, from the South in the 1950s; I am a first-generation northerner. I use the term first-generation deliberately—I didn't always think of it that way. I just knew that in my predominantly Black neighborhood and at my predominantly Black school (and by predominantly, I mean 99.9 percent), most of our parents had migrated from the South. In the first half of the 20th century, Cleveland was an industrial town; steel mills and car manufacturing were the industries that especially attracted southern Black folks seeking jobs and relief from Jim Crow segregation.

Journalist and Pulitzer Prize winner Isabel Wilkerson's *The Warmth of Other Suns: The Epic Story of America's Great Migration* helped me frame my family's story as one of migration that parallels immigration stories. According to Wilkerson, the Great Migration is perhaps the biggest underrepresented story of the 20th century. Over six decades, six million Black Southerners left the

South in search of new lives, including my parents and the parents of many of my friends.

Wilkerson's book honors this massive movement of people doing what migrants and immigrants throughout history have done—pick up and leave all you know for a better life for you and your children. To move to cities and towns where your labor is wanted, but you are not. Not your culture and your sensibilities and your story. Migration stories are complex stories of hope, courage, fear, and genuine danger. These are also stories of loss: separation from extended family and faith communities, separation from language and customs, separation from the earth as many rural folk were pushed into urban centers. These stories created the context that shaped me as I grew up in an all-Black neighborhood and attended Black public schools. I was also shaped by growing up in an intentionally interracial church within this all-Black setting.

My normal church experience was that of Black and white Christians worshipping together, studying scripture together, and doing church business together. This is unusual now, extremely rare in the middle of the 20th century. As a kid, while I knew racism was a thing, my experience and the model set by my elders led me to grow up thinking that friendship was an important key to unlocking America's "trouble" with race – clearly, I did not yet have an analysis of structural racism. So, as a child, I was also appropriately ignorant of what it cost my elders, Black and white, to be church together. Some families left the church rather than participate in this venture. Those who stayed formed and committed themselves to a community which did not avoid or downplay race, culture, or ethnicity. Despite what outsiders may have imagined, this was not a whitewashed Black church, nor a white church cosplaying as Black. This community nurtured and celebrated Black identity and culture and acknowledged the existence of racism and the effect it had on people in our church and our neighborhoods while also unapologetically teaching and preaching Anabaptist theology. This is certainly not to say that it was not done easily or perfectly—how could it be?

My grounding in this place helped me later identify basic, important, and often-overlooked questions that need to be asked when aiming to do any kind of justice/anti-oppression work. First, who is here, and who is not? Sometimes this is the only question asked, and it only leads to how to get more of "them" in the door (whoever "they" are). It's more useful to ask:

- Who gets to be seen (and in what capacity)?
- Whose stories are heard and believed?
- Whose stories are valued as part of what makes us a community?

While my elders may not have asked these exact questions, they tended to them in their way. Their goal was to be a visible representation of what they understood to be God's vision for humanity by saying who we want to be, who is not here, and why. It was an attempt to be genuinely countercultural by not only offering a vague "welcome" to one another but also doing the hard work of being an interracial community in a society that actively, without apology, opposed such communities. They were bold in a way that was rare in the 1950s.

This community planted the seed for the work that consumed most of my working life. I talk about this to bear witness to the hard work and the long-term commitment necessary to sustain such a vision. It is not a formula that works in every setting or a prescription for what all groups should do. But it is a testimony of my understanding of what helped me learn, grow into, and act upon what it means to move in ways that lead to equity and justice.

To seriously engage in anti-oppression work calls for commitments to truth-telling and accountability. The model of antiracism training I practice in community with others always begins with truth-telling that recounts a history of intentional racism in the US baked into the first structures and institutions created when this land was blatantly and unapologetically committed to the notion of white supremacy. It is an ugly history that must be named without apology for the naming.

A commitment to accountability means we then ask: now that we know our historical context and what we have inherited, what shall we do? How do we hold ourselves accountable for creating new systems and structures that do not uphold the notion of white supremacy? Who gets to be seen, whose stories are heard, whose stories are believed and valued? The answers to these questions depend upon the social location of the ones answering. Account-ability looks different and requires different kinds of commitments from different people. It raises questions that institutions claiming an anti-oppression identity should sort out and consider. To whom does the institution and its agents hold itself accountable? The marginalized community? The board of directors? The donors? What happens when these communities are in philosophical tension with one another? This level of complexity can make or break a predominantly white institution's "success" in claiming and acting out an anti-racist/anti-oppression identity.

This resistance work is exhausting and trauma-inducing and is consistently under threat from generation to generation. It is work that cannot hope to be sustained without making space for restora-tion—self and community care. This includes care for those who don't even realize they have been wounded.

In 1935, W.E.B. du Bois defined whiteness as a "public and psychological wage" that worked strategically to get poor whites to align with whiteness over and against solidarity with poor Black people. What du Bois knew then, we see as a continued, extraordi-narily successful tactic in the first quarter of the 21st century. The history of whiteness is also aligned with American Christianity, with religious imagery, ideologies, movements, and tropes that solidify notions of white superiority. The Doctrines of Discovery and Manifest Destiny justified exploration, colonization, and the transatlantic slave trade. These elements comprise the DNA of the United States and have impacted the purpose and mission of educational institutions—who teaches and where, who gets to learn, and where?

My mother raised me to see the beauty, resilience, and power of Blackness (with a capital B) in a world where "whiteness" has long held the presumption of humanness, of being civilized, the 'of-courseness' of being a citizen, owning property, having the right to vote (reserved at first for white men only)—the presumption of competence. The dominance of the white body, with all of its presumptions, conversely conferred the opposite presumptions on Black bodies. These presumptions enforce a particular vulner-ability.

In peace studies and justice work, we recognize vulnerability's necessity. Our work does not engage intellect alone. For Black and Brown-bodied people in predominantly white institutions, that vulnerability shows up in specific ways. This has meant teaching in a way that opens me up to criticisms that I need to discern daily, even moment by moment, if and how to address. I cannot teach as though the subject matter is sterile and unconnected to my life and the lives of my students, although it may be connected to our lives in significantly different ways. I know that to be "hearable," I need to foster a somewhat dispassionate tone and distance myself from my passion and my own pain. The power of whiteness and its paradoxical fragility matter for my ability to talk about and teach about race. The term "white fragility" was coined by Robin DiAngelo to explain the absence of the idea of whiteness and its corresponding privileges in discourse about race, and renders discussions of race intolerable for white people, often triggering anger, fear, and guilt rather than constructive conversa-tion. I have experienced the way fear/anxiety/resentment continues to hamper the ability to have honest discussions about the history and meaning of whiteness. Those conversations matter; our movements need white people to show up and do their work.

But as whiteness continues to be an unmarked norm, discussions about whiteness too often remain lodged in the academy and self-identified social justice communities. Even within the academy, these discussions must be mainstream; they must live where most people live. Our task in higher ed is to do what we can to make this possible, equipping ourselves and our students to do the work. This, of course, becomes more and more difficult in the face of the current dismantling of anti-oppression and humanitarian efforts. Yet, this is an indication of how very powerful such education can be.

A few years ago, I worked with two white students on a project that investigated how white people understood and talked about their whiteness. Initiated by the students, they were interested in discovering how Christian communities, explicitly or implicitly, shaped the meaning of white identity. The students began by investigating their own individual "whiteness narratives," starting with these questions and then asking the same of their subjects:

Discuss your racialized identity – that is, your identity as a white person by answering the following questions:

- Where did you spend your childhood and teenage years? If in the U.S., describe the racial composition of the place(s) you lived. This should be as best you remember it. It might be interesting to see if you can discern the actual demographics compared to what you remember. What does it mean to be racially identified as "white"— what does this designation mean to you? Do you/have you used the word "white" to describe yourself? Why or why not? Is there a word that you prefer? What is it, and why do you like it?

o How did you come to understand the meaning of whiteness? That is, how was race discussed in your family of origin? Was it discussed? Or did you learn about race by what was not said?

- Who taught you what it means to be a white person? This is admittedly a complicated question and has to do with being able to understand the role and function of white identity in a racially diverse and racially divided societal context. Remember, this is about what you were taught about your identity, not what you were taught about other people (although what you were taught about others may have been significant for your identity). Think about direct and indirect messages from family, friends, school, media, etc.

- Was race discussed at church? How and why (as best as you can recall)? What do you remember being said about whiteness and white people in church?

The student researchers interviewed a small sample from predominantly white Mennonite contexts to hear how they understood and acted out their own racial identities. Interviewees were solicited and selected from congregations and Mennonite institutions that had been part of a network of churches participating in anti-racism training over the preceding 20 years. Choosing from this pool allowed them to talk with people who have had some level of experience talking and thinking about race from a faith-based perspective, with a focus not only on individual opinions and attitudes, but also on systems and institutions.

The students were not surprised to find that for most of the respondents, their identity as Mennonite had more salience than whiteness did. Most of them had *not* had conversations about race, and particularly about being white, in their churches. Respondents in their 20s and 30s were much more accustomed to conversations about race, although discussions about whiteness were still rare in their churches and homes. This underscores the need for white institutions and agencies to normalize conversations about race, address "white fragility" and comfort, and build the capacity to sustain conversations in institutional settings to address policies and procedures that support white supremacy. This inquiry matters and is a critical part of our collective resistance, especially in the race of the rise of white Christian Nationalism. I consider the broad categories of resistance, resilience, and radical love as pillars that uphold a vision for a future dreamed of and worked toward by my ancestors.

RESISTANCE

Just as oppressive systems are institutionalized, so too must be our resistance. Resistance to white supremacy and empire has always been a part of our history, although too little told and too often suppressed. This history parallels the struggles of marginalized and oppressed people across the globe: those who have been forcibly removed from their homelands, those whose populations have been decimated by genocide, the victims of apartheid, and all of their descendants. Their pain, suffering, and deaths built the country's wealth, and the desire to keep that wealth and the supposed comfort it brings hold oppressive systems in place, necessitating the need for long-term, sustained strategies of resistance. We follow in the footsteps and stand on the shoulders of those who resisted by rebellion, refusal to cooperate, and other forms of activism. We recognize that resistance comes in many forms—it is not always loud or visible. We regret not honoring different forms of resistance because they didn't look like ours or because of what we aspired to do and be in the movement. And we mourn the time lost when, in our communities of struggle, we have disagreed with each other's tactics, perspectives, and even how the systems used our multiple oppressions to fight with each other instead of fighting white supremacy, patriarchy, heterosexism, capitalism, and a host of other isms.

RESILIENCE

Despite continued efforts to beat down and exterminate Black, Brown, and Indigenous people, Maya Angelou proclaimed, "Still, I rise."[3] Historic policies like the Indian Removal Act, the Chinese Exclusion Act, and federal and state fugitive slave laws show how blatantly and unapologetically legislators sought the destruction of people of color if we did not remain confined to the places and roles that served white supremacy and capitalism. Despite the plans that displaced us and destroyed many of our ancestors, some of us are still here, and we carry the essence of those we lost in our bodies. We trust the wisdom of our bodies and the space we occupy between our ancestors and descendants. We give energy to discerning the work for our time and place—where we are on the continuum of what and who we have been (ancestors) and what and who we will be (descendants). When I don't know that what I've done matters—the small things and the large—I remember all the large and small movements and moments that have allowed me to be here now. To paraphrase Alice Walker, my activism is the rent I pay, the debt I owe to those who come after I am gone.

RADICAL LOVE

Radical love calls us to keep our humanity and connectedness to the created order centered. It calls us to recognize that we are created from love and for love and that joy is our birthright. Even when fighting for our lives, we know in our bones that we persist because we have chosen not to let the forces of destruction win. In

---

3. Angelou, Maya. "Still I Rise" in And Still I Rise, Random House, 1978, pg. 41.

the moments we cannot continue, we depend upon those who have the energy for it that day. Radical love is not a mushy, gushy feeling that waters down or diminishes the devastating effects of oppression on our bodies, minds, and spirits. Instead, it refuses to let our bodies, minds, and spirits leave this existence without recognizing our fundamental, essential beauty and worth. These find their expression in what and how we create, who and how we love, and our refusal to let the bastards win. "Radical love is love amplified. It is love with a double shot of social justice. ...It's about courage, not fear, and a commitment to others."[4]

We are not the first, and we won't be the last, to try to fashion a beautiful, livable life that is clear-eyed about the state of the world. Our success depends upon hearing and telling our stories of resistance, resilience, and radical love.

I started writing the musings that would become this book in 2022, two years after a global epidemic forced a lockdown and protests over the murder of George Floyd rocked city after city across the country and then the world. Wars, genocides, and numerous political upheavals followed on the heels of one another in a seemingly whirlwind fashion. (In the various drafts of this chapter, the list of breaking news items began to outpace my ability to keep track without seeming to lift one atrocity over any other regarding their impact on human life and welfare.) The ability to have immediate knowledge of events around the world intensifies feelings of helplessness and belief in the inevitability of the world collapsing in on itself due to human destruction of each other and the planet. Perhaps this is so. Yet, it helps to think about the long arc of history, which contains story after story of human destruction, yes, but also story after story, evidence after evidence,

---

4. Dana Stachowiak. Living, Breathing, and Teaching with Radical Love: What it Means, What You Need, and Where to Start. The Educator Collaborative Blog, November 11, 2016. https://community.theeducatorcollaborative.com/living-breath ing-and-teaching-with-radical-love-what-it-means-what-you-need-and-where-to-start/

of the human capacity to rise repeatedly. Teaching for liberation means imagining the world we want to live in and practicing living in that world.

2

RESISTANCE

THE FIRST TIME I READ *THE BRIDGE POEM* BY DONNA KATE Rushin, I felt *seen*. It seems I've always moved between diverse groups who traveled in their own specialized orbits: bookish nerds, theater people, feminists, and church folk, to name a few. I know and connect with all of the kinds of groups Rushin referenced: family members of different generations, white feminists and Black church folks, ex-hippies, and Black separatists and artists—all folks in my world who couldn't understand each other and sometimes didn't understand me:

Then
I've got to explain myself
To everybody

I do more translating
than the Gawdam UN[1]

---

1. Donna Kate Rushin. "The Bridge Poem" in *This Bridge Called My Back: Writings*

Many people can probably relate. Those who travel between communities, perhaps wondering if they really fit into any of them, have something important to offer. As Rushin writes, being a translator is exhausting, but a necessary part of justice work. Now more than ever, people need to be equipped and prepared to move within and between groups as we build and strengthen coalitions. In 1981, Bernice Johnson Reagon spoke about coalitions at the West Coast Women's Music Festival. In looking ahead to the turn of the century, Reagon cautioned the festival goers against the comfort of having a space that is "yours only." These places, she noted, could be very nurturing or very destructive. While acknowledging the need for nurturing spaces/places (like a women's festival), Reagon cautioned against insularity, in large part because it prevents coalition building. There needs to be room for both a home base for safety and nurture, and coalitions that amplify our power.

> Coalition work is not work done in your home. Coalition work has to be done in the streets. And it is some of the most dangerous work you can do. And you shouldn't look for comfort. Some people will come to a coalition and they rate the success of the coalition on whether or not they feel good when they get there. They're not looking for a coalition; they're looking for a home! They're looking for a bottle with some milk in it and a nipple, which does not happen in a coalition. You don't get a lot of food in a coalition. You don't get fed a lot in a coalition. In a coalition you have to give, and it is different from your home. You can't stay there all the time. You go to the coalition for a few

---

from Radical Women of Color, Cherrie Moraga and Gloria Anzaldua, Watertown, Persephone Press, 1981.

hours and then you go back and take your bottle wherever it is, and then you go back and coalesce some more.[2]

Coalition work involves inviting people to learn about themselves, each other, and the wider world to build mutual understanding necessary for cooperation and collaboration. Liberation is not the work of only one person or one group, but it does depend on us bringing our whole selves.

My identity as a Black woman mediates my experience of all my other identities. Race has shaped my context; it shapes how I see myself and how I am seen. This double consciousness, although well documented, is baffling and merits accusations of divisiveness to those who deny the salience of race. Those folks would see me as less of a bridge and more of a roadblock to a race-neutral utopia. Race neutrality has never been a reality in the U.S., and the lack of attention to how race matters has been to the severe detriment of peace studies as a discipline and peace work.

Understanding the role my Black identity plays in my life matters in peace and justice education. Most of my working life has been in predominantly white, Christian faith-based spaces and calls for healthy doses of bridge work. I have navigated these spaces well (I hope) because of the communities that nurtured me. I witnessed people at home, school, and church being conscious about how they related to people across boundaries of race and class. What happens within our communities is just as important: marginalized folks create and practice strategies like code-switching, whisper networks, and spaces like "the Black table" to thrive. In addition, many of the adults in my life demonstrated daily how they valued Black people: the elementary school teacher who had our class memorize poetry from the Harlem Renaissance, the

---

2. Reagon, B. J. "Coalition Politics: Turning the Century" in Home Girls: A Black Feminist Anthology, B. Smith, ed. New York: Kitchen Table Press, 1983, pgs. 356-368.

gospel choir director in high school who pushed us to excellence, and my mother, an early childhood educator whose advocacy for Black kids included co-founding a small publishing company that published Black history books for children, and founding a community theater that produced plays about the African American experience. A lifelong community theater buff, my mom cast me in my first play at age 13: Langston Hughes' *Simply Heavenly* in which I played Arcie, the town drunk. (Thanks, Mom!) These were large and small acts of daily resistance during the last gasps of legalized segregation and the continuing fight for civil rights. They were my first lessons in justice and social change.

My faith community was also part of this education. Discussions about race were not limited to the quality of interpersonal relationships but about how racism impacted life in everyday ways, like why the busted streetlights and potholes in poor Black communities didn't get fixed as quickly as they did in white communities, or whether they got fixed at all. It was about the availability of decent food, good public transportation and the state of public schools. I watched my mom and other adults in the neighborhood be consistently involved in local political campaigns and neighborhood improvement activities.

For a number of years before moving into higher ed, I worked as a peace and justice educator for several church agencies, and it had always made sense to me that talking about race/racism was part of that. I saw racism as a force that contributed to much of the violence in the world. I served as a pastor for several years in the church that raised me, and eventually, I took on a campus pastor position at my current school and was occasionally asked to teach classes. In the midst of teaching and continuing to do anti-racism work with organizations, I went back to school myself, this time for a Ph.D. I went back and forth for a long while before taking the plunge—was I too old? Did I have what it takes to complete it? Did I want to spend the resources of time (especially time I took from family) and money to do it? Ultimately the answer was yes. It was hard, and I do not take the accomplishment lightly.

Formal education in the U.S. was historically limited to the elite, with university education in particular being expressly for wealthy white men. Criminalizing literacy was an essential way to keep enslaved people in their places. It was illegal to teach an enslaved person to read or write—violators suffered whipping, amputation, or worse. After emancipation, Black Codes and Jim Crow continued to withhold education through taxes, inadequate funding, and, of course, violence. Even after the Supreme Court declared public school segregation unconstitutional, vicious backlash persisted. This is how deep and normalized it was: while Ruby Bridges is perhaps the name best known, she and other Black students who were the first to integrate schools required federal protection from white adults bent on keeping schools white (yes, they even carried signs saying 'Keep Our Schools White'). Bridges endured an entire school year as the only student in her classroom. This history and its legacy represent the resistance power of the adults who then and now made space for Black kids to learn, flourish, and love their Blackness. Many also recognized integration was not always in the best interest of Black folk and advocated for protected Black spaces, calling into question the "benefits" of going into places where we are not wanted.

My education is a resistance story. It is a resistance story for all who paved the way to make it possible and resistance to the narrative that said to my ancestors, "You may know nothing except that which we tell you." Keeping (or trying to keep) knowledge from an entire group of people supported how anti-Blackness became a part of U.S. culture. It is not only the denying of access to education but the simultaneous denial of Black humanity and value—teaching that Black people had/have no history, no culture, no artistry, nothing. In the 21st century, when the average person has a surface-level knowledge and understanding of Black history, it's almost easy to understand people who opine that we are just looking for something to be offended by. When the knowledge base is deeper and more accurate, it's easy to see how and why; there is so much shock and downright anger when a Black person takes up space and dares to be seen. To illustrate how casually and boldly this shows up in the present day, I show my students a screenshot of white people's social media reactions when they realized the character Rue in *The Hunger Games* movie was played by a Black actor. More recently, *The Little Mermaid*, a live-action film, and the "Dr. Who" series received similar vitriol when Black people played the title characters. Mainstream culture (read: whiteness) could not imagine Blackness centered in popular culture. We see it showing up in education in so many ways, especially the inability of many people to even imagine capable scholarship and expertise coming from Black people, other people of color, and other marginalized groups.

Our school's Black Student Union hosts an annual cookout to which everyone on campus is invited. The first one I went to was a great event with good food, music, and dancing. I posted on social media about how happy I was for this Black-centric event. A comment from a white person under my post expressed the hope that "the college cared about all of its students." Now, because I knew this person, I was 98% certain that the comment was not meant to be mean-spirited or provocative, but it bothered me. It was another reminder of how much and how often white people are conditioned to complain or at least question the necessity of Black spaces, and the irony of how most of the history of this country illustrates the hyper concern with keeping us out/separate, but now questions the development of our own spaces. This country has never known what to do with Blackness outside of what Dr. King called the "thingification"[3] of Black people. It is a love/hate relationship that can be traced through cultural artifacts

---

3. Thingification was a term used by Martin Luther King, Jr., to indicate the dehumanization of Black people in America.

like postcards, ceramics, and, of course, minstrel shows in which white folks play with and parody Blackness, or more current media representations that confine Blackness to palatable configurations. These artifacts are easily found in vintage and antique stores around the country, and I have an entire photo album stored in my phone of ones I've seen personally. These representations showed an intense fascination with representing Black life within specific rigid confines and then using those representations for entertainment. The 21st century has not escaped this legacy, and Black presence in education and industry are still under attack.

While literacy and equal opportunity for schooling have systematically been denied to Black people, the formal education system in the U.S. has also functioned as a way of solidifying a class hierarchy. Formal schooling was initially restricted to wealthy families; the need for an educated and more compliant workforce led to compulsory education. Access was eventually given to non-wealthy families because the economic system needed people with the ability to read, write, and do math, so school became available and required for children of all classes. Streams of immigration made it necessary to teach "American" values.

Despite attempts to limit who could be educated and what they could learn, Black people have fought for the right to knowledge. The slave narrative genre shows some of the most profound resistance in enslaved people's accounts of their own lives, whether written by themselves or narrated to another literate person, often a white person who vouched for the account in the introduction or forward. The enslaved person's narrative frequently chronicled the attainment of literacy, generally by subterfuge.

Education is power and is a mediator of power in many ways. In the 21st century, while the U.S. is more diverse, schools remain highly racially segregated. A recent study indicated white parents support neighborhood schools if the neighborhood school is white; if the school is Black, white parents then support school choice. Investigative journalist Nikole Hannah-Jones calls this phenomenon "curated diversity," which is a diversity that still holds white students in the majority. "White Americans, in general, are willing to accept about the ratio of Black Americans at large: 10 to 15 percent."[4]

The fight over who gets taught what, and where, continues. In addition to skills and critical thinking, schools teach the norms and values of a society and play a part in socializing individuals into their identity as part of a people group. While the early production and distribution of textbooks standardized things like spelling and word pronunciation, they also endorsed patriotism and religion. Moreover, textbooks sanitized the era of enslavement and taught the racial hierarchy. Illustrations showed a linear progression of "primitive" to civilized man (sic) with Indigenous people and Africans on the far left and Europeans on the far right, an up/down hierarchy with white men at the top, or "the races of man" with a white man in the center and other racial groups in a circle around him. They gave a physical representation that mirrored the racial ideology and included negative stereotypes of Native Americans and other non-European groups or those who had not assimilated into whiteness yet, like Italians and other southern Europeans.

While law segregated schools until 1954, the residential patterns that were established kept segregation alive. Numerous cities responded to a need to address the growing population of African Americans moving in and the corresponding white panic. A so-called "Negro invasion" of middle-class Black people leaving poor neighborhoods spurred new legislation to firmly establish separate white and Black neighborhoods. This was not just the South; as Black people migrated to the North, so did opposition to Black bodies in previously-white spaces across the nation.

By 1930, most large cities with a significant Black population

---

4. Dianna Douglas, "Are Private Schools Immoral?," The Atlantic, January 10, 2018, https://www.theatlantic.com/education/archive/2017/12/progressives-are-undermining-public-schools/548084/.

had established exclusive areas where Black people could live. The machinery of segregation became more sophisticated with tactics like restrictive covenants—contractual agreements among property owners that restricted the sale or lease of the property to a Black family for a specified period, usually 99 years. These practices depended upon agreement with a racial hierarchy ideology that positioned African Americans at the bottom. By the 1940s, residential segregation in the North was increasingly justified by "free market" language and the right of white citizens to protect the value of their property.

This legacy of segregation persists and continues to have ongoing detrimental effects. Because schools are funded through tax dollars, a poor city will have schools lacking essential resources like books and more experienced teachers. But it's not just specifically "educational" resources—the condition of the school itself makes a difference. For instance, children from schools that lack functioning heating and cooling have been noted to fare poorly on standardized tests, and thus a vicious cycle is perpetuated.

Disparities in health care similarly document a legacy of historic and contemporary harms. The 19th-century surgeon J. Marion Sims, known as the "father of modern gynecology," honed his craft (and made his name) by experimenting on the bodies of enslaved Black women, who he (and others) believed did not feel pain in the same manner as white women. The belief that Black people do not feel pain in the same way as white people was part of the justification of slavery (are Black people human?) and has remarkable staying power. Recent studies indicated that medical students and residents (people trained in the workings of the human body) believe African Americans have thicker skin and less sensitive nerve endings than whites and, therefore, do not have the same pain management requirements.

We could see Sims as someone who stands apart from the time and place he was located, but that would be a mistake. Dr. Sims did not do his work under the cover of night or hidden in a basement or dark alley. Instead, because of the context in which he lived, where Black and female bodies were objects to be used and not considered to be fully human or bodies that anyone had to be accountable to, he was able to do his work without censure. Until recently, Sims was lauded as a hero for his medical advances, and there continue to be defenders of his work.

More well-known is the Tuskegee experiment. In the 1930s, poor Black men were studied, without their consent, to learn how untreated syphilis affected the body. The men were promised "special free treatment," including overnight stays at the hospital and food while they stayed. They were told they were being treated for "bad blood." The medical community knew at the time of the experiment that penicillin was an effective treatment; the men were specimens to see what happened when the disease was allowed to run its course. Local doctors who took part in the study had to agree that they would not tell the men that their disease had a name—syphilis—and that it was curable.

In the 1950s, biopsied cancer cells from Henrietta Lacks, an African American woman, were the basis of a cell line that has proven critical to cervical cancer research. Lacks was receiving treatment at Johns Hopkins, the only hospital that would treat Black patients in her area. While Ms. Lacks received treatment, she and her family did not receive full disclosure regarding what was done with the cells harvested from her body and how much the medical community was benefiting from it. Lacks' family was not compensated for the use of her cells for profit by drug companies until 2023, when the family settled a lawsuit. It is yet another instance of using Black bodies as commodities for financial and social gain at the expense of those same Black bodies. While we can and should look at these examples and many others with dismay and outrage, a critical commonality in these cases is how typical, business-as-usual they were.

This history illustrates how Black bodies are seen and valued, but it is not a history that is done. Black bodies continue to be thingified and in need of a complex series of standardized ways to be controlled. Gender, class, and sexual orientation complicate the dynamic further.

Black women's bodies were and are seen as immoral and irresponsible. The shaping of the U.S.'s current patriarchal, capitalist framework was built upon the foundation of the trans-Atlantic slave trade and its ensuing institution of forced labor. This foundation was solidified by legalized and de facto racial segregation. These racialized and gendered public policies continued to perpetuate the belief that Black women are not women (because we are Black), our bodies are not human (because they are not white), and we are not allowed agency. We do not matter unless we are needed as scapegoats for societal problems.

A 1990s opinion column by a prominent columnist for the Boston Globe was accompanied by a graphic depicting several Black figures grabbing for cash and an Afro-coiffed woman in the center holding a baby who is also reaching for cash. The column and its illustration were just one among many that served to reaffirm the myth that the face of a welfare recipient is an immoral Black woman who, in turn, teaches her children to be immoral and that "we" need to teach "them" some values. These articles were extending the decades-earlier specter of then-presidential candidate Ronald Reagan's "welfare queen," a Black woman who flouted a lavish lifestyle on the backs of hardworking taxpayers. (Linda Taylor, the woman to whom Reagan referred, was later revealed to have been a white woman, according to the census record.)

I love being a Black woman and was taught from little on up that I come from beauty, strength, and magnificence. I love myself, and I love my people. I have plenty of joy in my life. And yet, a lifetime of learning all of this history, knowing it, and teaching it routinely makes me feel sad, angry, and often hopeless about the future that our children will inherit despite the blood, sweat, and tears of generations of people. I've seen in the classroom and workshops how anger—my own and that of my students and workshop participants—either fuels the desire to do something or deflates the energy to do anything. Many people have discovered that there is power ignited when we acquire language that makes it possible to articulate what our bodies and spirits have known all along: that systemic violence, like racism, operates in concert with an actual grand scheme. For racism, the grand scheme is the perpetuation of white supremacy. For sexism and misogyny, it is the perpetuation of patriarchy. In all forms of violence, the purpose is to provide some benefit to one group at the expense of others. Knowing this helps clarify why systemic violence remains so entrenched and why it self-perpetuates, generation after generation. It's not just a matter of people's personal prejudices that must be unlearned and overcome.

The anger at these realities provides a powerful ignition for fighting back, for resistance, but resistance can't run on rage alone. It is too costly for our mental, physical, and spiritual health. It is costly to our relationships with our loved ones. Anger certainly and appropriately has its uses, but it cannot be the whole of how we work against the systems of oppression because those systems are in it for the long haul. They intend to be embedded in our culture so profoundly that these notions are normalized, even in the games we play.

I learned about a game called Ghettopoly while researching the portrayal of Black people in popular culture for one of my classes. Created in 2002, the game is a parody of the board game Monopoly and plays on stereotypical notions of an American ghetto and the people who live there. According to the game, the features of the ghetto include pimps, hoes, crack houses, and carjacking, to name a few. After vigorous protest, the game was stopped from being sold by retailers like Urban Outfitters but continues to be marketed by its creator. This game (and many others) provides even more examples of how complex histories are realized in present realities and continue perpetuating ideas about who people are and, more importantly, how they should be treated. Indeed, some people who spend their good money on this game think it is just fun and does not harm any actual people. If questioned about their participation in racist stereotyping, they might point at Black people who think the game is funny or maybe even bought one themselves, much in the way people who not Black are justify using the n-word because some Black people do. Ghettopoly is just one item in a long line of racist portrayals of Black people, Black life, and Black culture. They began as justification for the enslavement of Black people, in the same ways that stereotypes against Indigenous people justified the theft of their lands and the attempts at genocide. They paved the way for legislated segregation, the historical and contemporary over-policing of movement, and mass incarceration.

Music as an art form reflects and shapes culture. Making music is part of being human and part of what keeps us healthy—recent brain science has shed light on the powerful influence of music on individual mental health and how making music together creates powerful bonds in communities. Most people today acknowledge the common roots of the blues, R&B, and what has come to be known as country music. In 2024, the issue of culture, race, and music came to the fore through country music and who has the right to perform it. While not a new conversation, it sheds important light on the ways racism and anti-Blackness are embedded. Any group's music is a story of cultural influences. Being influenced by other cultures is to be expected. We must consider the music industry and follow the money in a capitalist society. We must also consider who benefits and who is included/excluded. At all levels, we must consider who is at the table and how they got there.

The term "Jim Crow," the label given to the system of racial segregation that affected pretty much all of life in post-slavery society, comes from the minstrel music era in the U.S. Minstrel shows were a popular form of entertainment in which white people donned blackface and performed stereotypical and racist caricatures of Black people for the amusement of other white people. These productions and their artifacts were also political; they were propaganda against the abolitionist movement. The performances defended enslavement by presenting denigrating stereotypes of Blacks who supposedly needed the civilizing influence of the institution. Enslaved Black people were commonly portrayed as happy and content with their lot in life, and terrified of life outside of the plantation without the guidance and "protection" of their masters. Banjos came to America with kidnapped Africans and were used in these shows. Some scholars note the use of the instrument in minstrel shows might be why Black people eventually distanced themselves from it, as a rejection of the shows and their nostalgia for the old South.

The music and entertainment industries became vehicles that helped cement social, cultural, and economic gulfs between Blacks and whites, resulting in supposedly racialized music genres, which are vigorously policed. Today's "country music" was first called hillbilly music, a category that included several genres, including bluegrass and gospel. This was music performed and enjoyed across racial lines. But record companies and related industries realized that promoting music for specific racial audiences diversified income possibilities, perpetuated the notion that racial identity was a critically important marker, and encouraged white people to place strict boundaries around "their" music. This is the power of institutional racism.

The stereotypes that emerge from this kind of history are meant to say, "This is what Black people are—danger, stay away," so that something as communal and human as sharing music becomes a line that people are told not to cross. We know that people say our communities are devoid of anything good or beautiful (even while consuming the products of our labor), but we also know there IS beauty, strength, and joy and those things have sustained our people across the diaspora during the hardest of times. And yes, we have reclaimed some things meant to demean and belittle us and turned them on their heads. You see, our joy, too, is our resistance.

Black people have been nurtured in communities in which generations of folk learned and taught each other how to live within the context of psychic, psychological, and physical pain and develop ways to resist and exist within those contexts. Yes, there have been unhealthy responses to this painful history, born from trauma. There have been and continue to be calls to claim and reclaim Black joy, proclaim Black rest, and claim the right to be. To take up space and not apologize for needing rest and play. The Harlem Renaissance of the 1920s and 30s and the Black is Beautiful movement of the 1960s also claimed joy and the right to take up space any way we wanted. Each iteration is another reminder that to do so—to claim space and autonomy, to practice joy—takes intention and practice.

After years of doing anti-racism education and teaching peace and conflict studies at the college level, my own body began to tell me I was doing a pretty bad job at being intentional about joy. I could talk a good game about it, and I have long believed in the power of finding rest and seeking delight in life. I needed to do more resistance and resilience care. My work causes me to spend many hours a day reading about, thinking about, and talking about how humans have been and are horrible to one another, then shaping it into course curricula for my students and inflicting the information upon them. There is no way around learning about conflict and violence without immersing oneself in conflict and violence. And because we live in the real world, what we are reading and thinking about is simultaneously happening in our neighborhoods, our cities, our country, and across the globe. Things happen to us and to our families and to people who look like us and our families. While reading about historical atrocities, we hear about current ones instantly. We are doing this for a deep understanding of how systemic violence becomes a norm, how it is entrenched in systems, and how it persists because it ultimately benefits someone.

As an educator and an advocate for justice, I am committed to a classroom that supports learning for all. Some semesters, the political spectrum is broad and rife with potential for in-class clashes. Beyond politics, students are from different racial, ethnic, religious, class (and more, much more) backgrounds. To try to adopt professorial neutrality would be dishonest, and to ignore violent speech or behavior would be unethical and make me a participant in violence. I don't attempt to hide my perspectives. But I don't want my students to pretend to be other than who they are to try and please me, and I don't want them to be afraid of speaking and writing truthfully because they think they will get a bad grade.

Over the years, the racial diversity of our campus has significantly grown. In the early years of my teaching, a majority of my students were white; currently I may have 40 to 50% of students of color in a classroom. It is still rare for me to have African American students, as this is the lowest demographic on our campus. I well recall from my own undergraduate experience (and my experience as a professor) that it is hard to be the only or one of a very few, particularly when the subject of race comes up. It is a tall ask, especially for younger students, to possibly jeopardize their relationships with their peers, requiring them to do what older adults are unwilling or unable to do: talk about whiteness, about racism, about a young Black man who looked like their cousin being murdered in the streets by the police. Nor should the burden be on them to "help" others understand, to be used as object lessons. Students who are biracial with a white parent or those who have been trans-racially adopted bring unique experiences and concerns. Unreasonable and often cruel societal expectations make it challenging to separate the spectrum of their lived experiences, what we learn together about how race and racism historically and currently function in society, and also having a white parent and a white side of the family, or an entire White family, who were not or are not equipped to handle what their children are faced with. Too many folks still believe that not talking about race, not talking about difference, is the better way to go.

The complexity of racial identity is exacerbated by the sheer divisiveness of discussions around it. On the one hand, identity is personal, and all of us should claim the right to name who we are, how we see ourselves, and how we want to be seen. But the very idea of race was created to promote a hierarchy that benefited those at the top. Those social, economic, and political benefits make it important to continually reinscribe the meaning of race generation after generation, even if that meaning differs from place to place and group to group. For instance, there is the "one-drop" rule to trace any evidence of Black blood in a person and there is the "quantum blood" designation for Indigenous people. The one-drop rule that dictated Black ancestry meant that Black status was applied to a person no matter how non-Black they might appear. The sociological term *rule of hypodescent* says it all: a multiracial child is socially relegated to the "lower" status. "One drop" because the designation didn't mean just your parents or grandparents—that powerful drop of Black blood extended through generations. The rule of hypodescent was preceded during the era of legalized enslavement by the principle of *partus sequitur ventrem* ("that which is born follows the womb"): the legal status of the mother determined the status of the child, so an enslaved woman was effectively able to increase the amount of property owned by the slaveholder. The father's status was not a determinant, a convenient system indeed for slaveholders who raped and impregnated enslaved women.

A different system of racialization was imposed on Native folks: blood quantum measurements were used to determine Native American tribal membership and legal status in order to restrict who could claim Native identity and access associated rights and resources. The one-drop rule disregarded the complexity of mixed ancestry and imposed a binary racial classification. Blood quantum created a graduated system of racial identity based on fractional ancestry. Both systems illustrate the social construction of race and the ways racial classification has been used as a tool of control and dispossession.

These impositions of racial identity constructed within the boundaries of societal racial hierarchy have an impact on how race is understood within and across racial lines. They make clear how impossible it is to really "not see race" or "not make everything about race" as is often demanded of Black, Indigenous, and other people of color. Race historically determined whether or not you could be a citizen, own property, where you could and could not live, what job you could have, and where and how you could be educated. The ripples from the past reverberate today. They didn't just disappear when the laws or the mores changed. The attitudes and beliefs fostered under the racialization project persist and evolve.

Despite the oft-repeated prediction (or hope?) by some that eventually interracial relationships will produce a society of all one race and racism will be over, the reality is that the socialization of discouraging and, for much of this country's history, prohibiting such relationships runs deep. The fear of not being white or white adjacent enough fuels continues anti-Blackness that is perpetuated by white people and people of color, including Black people. However, historical amnesia prevents an understanding of how deeply embedded anti-Blackness has been and how it continues to reverberate and influence the culture at large.

Knowing, teaching, and learning these histories are acts of resistance. Resistance means honoring history. These acknowledgments are ways to start to repair the harm that was done. But hear this: it is not the responsibility of those who suffer the harm to do the repair. From my own experience and the stories of others, I know it is possible to touch the past in healing ways, at the least because they are a way of getting back stories that were taken. In particular, artists pave the way for this kind of healing. African

American artist and activist Michelle Browder invited the public to join her in creating the "Mothers of Gynecology" sculpture, commemorating the Black women who were experimented on by J. Marion Sims.[5] Created by discarded objects donated by the public, the monument depicts three women – Anarcha, Betsy, and Lucy. It honors them for the role they unwittingly played in advancing gynecological techniques. The Tuskegee Experiment's accountings and Henrietta Lacks' story have been told and memorialized in various mediums that allow the public to hear these stories, often for the first time.

We humans can build peace, and justice is something that can happen. Even so, I must revisit and recommit myself to these beliefs because I believe in telling the truth as best as I know it. If I didn't believe that this messed up world that is experienced so harshly by so many could change, I wouldn't teach and preach the things that I do. Yet, I don't believe these possibilities every day. Some days, I believe it because it gets me to put one foot in front of the other. Many other days, I believe it because I see people showing up and doing their work—justice-making liberatory works in action. I believe it because I look at the historical record and think about how my experience of being a Black woman in this country is different from my mother's and my grandmother's experiences. I know that change is possible, and we seek it when we do justice work even if we also know we will not see the fruits of our labor.

The hard truth is I have to believe it and live into that belief because I don't have the luxury of the choice not to. I have to keep showing up for myself and my students. I want to be someone who fans the flames of their hope, their quest for a world where they can flourish instead of being diminished. They are full of the same

5. Safiya Charles. Event Honors Enslaved Women Subjected to Gynecological Experiments in Alabama. Southern Poverty Law Center, March 1, 2024. https://www.splcenter.org/news/2024/03/01/event-honors-mothers-of-gynecology

kind of hope I had when I was twenty, a hope I recognize, and I honor its exuberant power. I often miss it. But I wouldn't trade this stage in my life and the things I've learned about being in the struggle for the long haul.

When I first began doing anti-racism work, my children were young, and our family lived in a multiracial neighborhood. We went to a multiracial church, the same church that I was raised in. I have never given up on the spark ignited in me simply by being in a community with people doing something that so many thought was impossible.

At the present moment, such hope seems foolish. My babies are adults now, with children of their own. I live with the fear of what might happen to them if someone feels they are "out of place" or "threatening." This fear and my love for them, my community, and the many co-conspirators who walk with me keep me going. When I need to step back to gather my wits, to refresh, or just to be, I know that other people are standing in—not in my place but theirs. We do this work together.

There is a well-worn adage that to understand the future means we must know the past, and it is once again critical when voices warn about the supposed dangers of examining the past or spread accusations that the past we wish to understand did not happen. Misunderstandings of Critical Race Theory and Diversity, Equity, and Inclusion initiatives are today's bogeymen, much as the Civil Rights Movement and other liberation movements were in the 1960s. While we laud the CRM and its heroes (many more names than Martin Luther King, Jr., and Rosa Parks), misty-eyed nostalgia can cloud the truth. Parks becomes mythologized as a tired seamstress who unwittingly sparked a freedom movement, and King's words are twisted into messages he never meant to convey. So our remembering is also a reclaiming of the truth. This reclaiming is and will continue to be costly.

Justice work is resistance work. It resists the idea that some of us were created as lesser beings, and it resists the systems and structures that perpetuate and sustain harmful hierarchies. For me, because I am still a person of faith, it is living fully into the notion that I am, and we are, created in the very image of the Divine. And the Divine is delighted to be in shalom community with us.

Remembering both manifestations of that embodiment is critical. In the summer of 2019, four generations of my family gathered together in Washington, DC, where my parents currently live. While there, we visited the Smithsonian Museum of African American History and Culture, a museum that encompasses so much of the beauty and the horror of the African and African American presence in the Americas (and is at this moment under threat of having its federal funding gutted). What stays with me the most is the small room, tucked away from the crowds, that contains the original casket of Emmett Till. Till was a 14-year-old Chicago boy who was lynched in Money, Mississippi, for allegedly whistling at a white woman. His mother, Mamie Till Mobley, had her child laid in the glass-topped casket so the world could see what happened to him. Till's body was exhumed for an autopsy many years after his death, and the original casket was donated to the museum by the family. I had long known Till's story. In that small room at the museum, where no photos are allowed per the family's request, I felt the enormity of Mamie Till Mobley's gift to the world—to look at the mangled body of her son, this son created in the image of the Divine. She dared us to see him and not look away.

I hold in balance how my Christian faith community has been vital to my grounding and the fact that Western Christianity is complicit in the teaching and supporting of white supremacy. The struggles of the 21st century for the soul of Christianity are not new. Harriet Jacobs and others explicitly named the cognitive dissonance of existing in an enslaved body and "belonging" to white Christians who bestowed all manners of abuse on them. The existence of slave narratives and other writings of Black people have expressed this dissonance over and over again. I was introduced to the poems of Paul Lawrence Dunbar and others in elementary school. Dunbar was born to formerly enslaved parents in Ohio in 1872. His poem "We Wear the Mask," likely his most famous, invites the reader directly into the psyche of a Black person in America who knows wearing a metaphorical mask is part of the key to survival. Pointedly, the speaker cries out to Christ in their pain while the world sees otherwise. Dunbar and other artists contextualized their religious convictions in ways that highlight the paradox embedded in Christianity's early history—a movement born of marginalized folks following a marginalized prophet. This movement becomes the religion of empires past and present. While there is a wide diversity of theological commitments and practices within the Black church in the U.S., that exists within a larger context of religious diversity—all Black folk are not Christian. For those of us who are, we need to wrestle with what it means to hold the complexity of our faith's history and how it, too, is embedded in white supremacy.

Resistance stories are necessary and powerful. It is imperative to ponder what will happen if we don't resist. Because it is lifelong work, I have learned to frame the question differently than our culture of "always do more" suggests. Instead of asking, "How much can I do?" or "How can I be more productive?" I now ask some version of this question, "How can I meet my obligations to this movement in ways that are not harmful to myself and others?"

We can make obligations to social justice movements that can be fulfilled if we are honest about what is possible for us at the given moment.

This means figuring out what things in my life will get my best energy, which means knowing everything can't get my best energy. It means setting priorities that will keep me faithful to my obligations, but it also means setting boundaries. The usual outward-facing obligations are work, school, family/friends, things that can more easily hold me accountable for showing up and following through.

The inward-facing obligations were the ones that are often

easier to ignore: mental and physical health (food/fuel, rest, exercise, creativity, joy). Because I live in the real world where many things are unpredictable, this also meant considering the things I can hold lightly. How do we/can we pass on a tradition of resistance?

In his 1901 biography *Up From Slavery*, Booker T. Washington spoke of 'taking off the mask' when the Civil War ended and freedom came. As the enslaved people waited for the word, he writes, "...there was more singing in the slave quarters than usual. It was bolder, had more ring, and lasted later into the night." Many of the songs they sang were about freedom, but the message carried in their hearts had to be hidden there. They dared not speak of freedom in the present world because to do so invited violence, so they masked their true desires. But when emancipation came, the mask was able to be discarded. They had a tradition of resistance.

Poet Dunbar's anguished cry to Christ shows a world that refused to see Black people's humanity and built legislation on the foundation of that refusal. In 1790, Congress enacted "that all free white persons who, have or shall migrate into the United States, and shall give satisfactory proof, before a magistrate, by oath, that they intend to reside therein, and shall take an oath of allegiance, and shall have resided in the United States for one whole year, shall be entitled to the rights of citizenship."[6] The racial dimension of this act was unquestioned—the relationship of whiteness to citizenship was assumed to be natural. There was much debate over other issues: the eligibility of Jews and Catholics, whether there should be a probationary period, if there should be character witnesses, etc. But there was no debate over whether citizenship should be open to those not white.

---

6. U. S. Laws, Statutes, Etc. *A bill to establish an uniform rule of naturalization, and to enable aliens to hold lands under certain restrictions. New-York, Printed by Thomas Greenleaf.* New York, 1790. Pdf. https://www.loc.gov/item/2020769535/.

The 1897 Dred Scott decision ruled that people of African descent—enslaved people and their free descendants—were not legal persons and could not be citizens of the U.S. According to the Court, the drafters of the Constitution viewed all Black people as "beings of an inferior order, and altogether unfit to associate with the white race, either in social or political relations, and so far inferior that they had no rights which the white man was bound to respect." This sentiment contributed to the notion of white supremacy as an irrefutable cultural norm that was upheld not only by the law but by religion, specifically Christianity. We do not have to draw too fine a line to trace the roots of the current era's pendulum swing toward white nationalist sentiments expressed in evangelical churches. The connection between culture, politics, and religion is long and deep. Decades of anti-racism work in predominantly white denominations that consider themselves progressive show how these ideas continue to be deeply embedded.

In 2020, when George Floyd was killed by a police officer in Minneapolis, Minnesota, the news sparked nationwide and global protest over the ongoing reality of the deaths of unarmed Black people at the hands of police officers. Because the pandemic had upended life for many people who found themselves confined to their homes, there was space to pay attention to racial violence in ways that had not been seen for decades. It disrupted the fantasy of a post-racial society that many progressive white people thought had been achieved. That summer, as I watched the way people processed Floyd's death, and the deaths of Breonna Taylor and Amaud Arbery earlier in the year (Taylor was asleep at home when police invaded the house, Arbery was jogging in a white neighborhood and was cornered and shot by men who didn't want Black people in it) and opined about race relations in the US and beyond, I felt sad and angry that the reality of racial terrorism seemed like brand new information for so many people, including people that I knew personally. In post after post on social media, people expressed their shock and dismay over issues I had been speaking, teaching, and writing about for nearly thirty years as if they were not the latest incidents in a long, continual line.

This was yet another reminder that this social justice work is indeed for the long haul, and long-haul strategies and education are critical parts of the work. While many of the strategies of the past need re-imagining, not all of them do. The non-knowledge of the past hampers us, and part of our work is to learn and relearn our history. This should not be done exclusively in the academy, but it must be there, though it must not be a solely academic enterprise. Inside the academy and without, it is critical to build on what we know from our histories, communities and cultures, just as systems of oppression form and reform generations of people into participating in and benefiting from unjust structures.

The student-led movements for desegregation in the 1960s are spiritual kin to the student-led movements of today for Black Lives Matter, for climate change, for water rights, and for the halting of genocide in so many places in this country and countries around the world. Students who were working for desegregation, starting with lunch counters, knew the campaign would be long. They knew this because they learned from other struggles and had their elders as mentors. They did not go it alone. The strategy for the lunch counter campaigns was, on the surface, straightforward. Students would go to the lunch counters and sit down. They knew they would be told they couldn't be served and that they would be ignored and harassed. And yet they kept coming, week after week. They also knew and planned for being arrested. They knew they would be met with verbal and physical violence. Their evening classes on nonviolent action not only taught them about the philosophy, but the action as well. They had practiced sitting, stone-faced and silent, as they were yelled at, called names, hit, and knocked down. They knew what they signed up for. And they kept coming, week after week. And their numbers grew.

Several years ago, I was contacted by a dean from a small religious college who was looking for someone to do a "diversity workshop" for the faculty at the beginning of the school year. The email (which I still have) said they needed someone to "work with faculty working with diverse students in the classroom." In my response email, I asked for specifics—what exactly did the dean understand such a workshop to be, and how much time were they willing to devote to it? This is always the starting point, especially when someone asks for "diversity" work, which is not the same as "anti-racism" work. In our email exchange, the dean wrote that their concerns were about "classroom management and managing behavioral issues/concerns. We have students from 11 different countries and a number from urban areas. Behaviors are different in downtown Chicago or Indianapolis. Classroom interactions and connecting with them (hopefully motivating them) are the important pieces."

My translation of this coded language was verified in our follow-up phone call, the "diverse" (read: Black) students that the school admitted were problems for the faculty. What the dean was really asking was (my paraphrase), "How can we teach these Black kids to behave in ways that are more palatable to our predominantly white campus?" It unfortunately reminded me of discussions I had been around for in other settings. People were concerned about all the extra work they were doing for Black students and other students of color who were identified as being not academically or socially prepared. In my experience students from all demographics had struggles. It was clear to me that problematic behavior and/or poor academic performance happened across the board; in fact, since there were more white students I had far more conversations with them than I did with students of color. Yet this was not a topic of concern.

I'm wary of anyone who says to me that Black and Brown students are problematic in ways that white students are not. I am especially testy about this when someone indicates that students of color are ill-prepared for college. Yes, this country has denied education and wealth to Black families, and underfunded and under-resourced schools in Black and Brown communities contribute to how those students arrive on our campuses needing more support. But I bristle at the students being blamed for this lack of preparation and being seen as an additional burden for the faculty, especially when it goes unrecognized that white students, too, struggle socially and academically.

In response to my conversation with the dean, I wrote a proposal (a bit spitefully) for a workshop that I could say yes to, knowing it would surely be rejected. I told the dean that my workshops on race (not diversity) generally lead participants into an investigation of their own racial identities and the narratives surrounding them within the context of a historically racialized country. From this foundation, I could help the faculty think about what this meant for their work. I suggested a few short readings to help prepare for the conversation and added that I would also compile resources for further reading after the workshop.

The full proposed schedule included:

- How We Got Here (The Social Construction of Race—Defining Terms and Setting Historical Context)
- Our Own Racial Stories and How They Matter
- Now That We're Here—What Do We Do?
  - Preparing to Teach
  - Classroom Dynamics
  - Advising Diverse Students (Today, I would change the language to Guidelines for White Faculty advising Black students. Always evolving.)

I didn't hear from the dean for several days. Then I received this short response: "Regina, thank you for your offer to assist (us) with diversity training. We have chosen a different provider at this time."

The way I handled this request happily represented a couple of things: an evolution in my teaching/action and the start of my taking seriously the need to prioritize my well-being. It also helped me clarify who my work was for and sidestep requests that did not fit into that box. In earlier years, I did accept requests like this and worked myself into a tizzy trying to balance what an organization wanted (and would pay for) and actual anti-oppression work. I had to unlearn the impulse to say yes to every request that came to me, because doing that did not further the work I was committed to. There are plenty of diversity folks out there. The real constraints of time, impending burnout, and the need for more clarity about what I would say yes to led to the three questions that guide me, and I offer to others as they are on this journey:

- What is my work?
- Who are my people?
- How will I sustain myself and my work?

The first question aids in clarifying my goals and weeding out what doesn't fit. It is also a philosophical question. The experience with the college wanting a diversity workshop that was really about "fixing" Black people clarified the easy "no." It led to me being able to say I don't do Racism 101. Too often, the invitation to speak to a book club, a Sunday School class, or a work team were really requests to come and convince people that racism was real – Racism 101. This simple clarification helped ease my decision-making and the guilt about saying no to some requests; I got over the guilt part quickly because invitations that are about an organization easing their guilt or checking off the "we fixed racism" box go against the kind of justice I want to see. Finally, it helps me make space for things in my life that are not work.

When I talk to my students and other folks about work in this context (what is my work?), it's not about my employment. I mean the work I must do, given who I am, the history I have inherited, and the context I live in. My work is grounded in my embodiment as a Black woman, a descendant of enslaved people who owes my existence to the survival of my ancestors and the insistence of my elders, blood and otherwise, that I know who and what I am in this world. It is vital that I honor those lives and the energy poured into me and my community. It is consciously taking on the responsibility to pay forward, do my part, and build on the foundation that was made for me.

But I also know that these responses to the massive responsibility to "show up" and do justice work are also embedded in a culture that lionizes overwork and weirdly rewards unhealthy and unsustainable practices. This is the opposite of what our movements for systemic change need to be. The harmful habits we develop come from various sources, including messages that tell us our worth is measured by how much we do, and how much of it is done for other people. Work centered on changing unjust systems and repairing/healing from the harm those systems have caused should not cause more harm! Grind culture grows from the soil of the white supremacist capitalist foundation that was built by stolen Black bodies on stolen Indigenous land. The myth of the self-made man depends upon endlessly regurgitating the idea that anyone who works hard enough can not only make it but achieve endless wealth and power. These powerful myths skirt over the real stories of how obscene wealth was created and hoarded. So yes, justice work is important and deserves our energy and passion and brilliance, but it must not come at the expense of the health of our bodies and psyches, or the strength and health of our families and communities. The balance requires thoughtful discernment. These are tools for long-term justice work.

Audre Lorde's essay "The Transformation of Silence into Language and Action" reminds us that our silences will not protect us—we are going to die either way. The essay was the text of Lorde's address at a 1977 Modern Language Association panel, in which she declared herself a Black woman warrior poet doing her work and pointedly asked those gathered whether they were doing theirs. Anticipating the pushback, she noted that our work is never done without fear.

I don't remember when I first came across Lorde's essay, but when I did find it, I recognized the truth and power of her words. When I worked for a predominantly white women's labor organization in my twenties, I saw that just because women could work together on gender issues, the same could not be said for working together across the lines of race. Because of our organization's target demographic (working-class women), class issues were definitely on the table, but the race analysis was sorely missing. The assumption was the familiar refrain - we are all in this together, so race is not an issue. Underneath was the playing out of the racial script written for us long ago.

So many of us come to this work because we are fighting for our lives, the lives of the people we love, and all those who will come after us. Our lived experience and history teach us that although this country wants us to love it, it does not love us back. There is a massive investment in denying the claims of racial terrorism, framing it as something abnormal and rare, and asserting that the past was unfortunate, but it is in the past, and we should just forget about it. And yet, justice is about the right relationships. These relationships are inside our movements; too many times, we fight each other. In the meantime, battles we thought were long won lay unfinished; the ground we thought we had gained rolled back. So, what do we do in the now? What is the strategy? Who are your people, and what will sustain you? From where you sit, what does justice look like in the day-to-day comings and goings? What does your discipline look like if you are an educator? Clean water? Access to education? A safe home? A safe campus? Who are the most vulnerable, and how are they included, represented, and made accountable?

The myths around how social justice work happens also keeps our history whitewashed. So much of what was said in the most visible part of the Civil Rights Movement by King and others has been watered down, misinterpreted, and even used against the Black community. Many figures that were part of that movement remain woefully unfamiliar to many. There were also missteps, flaws, and disagreements. We must be aware that as each generation does its work, that work will be looked back upon by future generations who will critique how we did what we did. For our time, let us not be afraid to make bold moves and radical connections.

Dr. King publicly identified the interrelatedness of the triple evils of racism, poverty, and militarism. They keep all of us from realizing "The Beloved Community," a term first used by theologian Josiah Royce and adopted by King. The Beloved Community means something attainable. Put simply, it is the idea that everyone can get along and share the earth's wealth. But it would take work. It would take skills. At the very least, it would take the acknowledgment of our common humanity (even those deemed inhuman) and our need for one another.

In *Pre-post Racial America: Spiritual Stories from the Front Lines,* Sandhya Jha writes: "A critical first step in building the Beloved Community is making sure no one has to be in perpetual fear for their lives. I think we sometimes overlook this step because we take it for granted... and while we continue to address that first step, maybe the next step is making sure everyone has some reason to hope for the future."[7] Jha goes on to say that not finding a way to hear one another's stories across difference will make us lose valuable time by having to rebuild the foundations of the Beloved Community over and over again. And we will lose members of our communities to frustration, to the watering down and diminishing of that vision, to being ignored and villainized. We reduce the vision and have to start from scratch, over and over and over again.

---

7. Jha, Sandhya Rani. Pre-Post-Racial America: Spiritual Stories from the Front Lines. St. Louis: Chalice Press, 2015, 15.

Perhaps the Beloved Community best begins in small ways. In sanctuaries. In classrooms. On dorm floors and in office suites. In these places, we find ourselves living our regular, daily lives. Perhaps for us, too, feats of extraordinary courage that break open that which we thought was unbreakable begin with small moments: paying attention to the world around us. Talking about it with our loved ones. Learning more by consciously seeking others with varying vantage points and different life stories. Being connected to and grounded in communities, unafraid to name injustice repeatedly. Beginning in small ways, yes, but refusing to stay small.

We don't revisit the stories of the past to rest upon days gone by, in the same way that we don't abandon our family, community, and faith narratives after we have heard them once. We tell our stories, the accurate, complicated human versions of them, to celebrate them, but also to equip us for the present. The threats of racism, poverty, and war are still with us. The work is not done.

Liberation is not achieved in isolation; it is achieved with community. It happens when we are informed and realize how oppressions are connected.

The Black women in my childhood neighborhood were champions of their communities. Most of them worked outside the home and still did countless hours of volunteer work, much of it in the church. My mother got involved in local politics because of the conditions in our Cleveland neighborhood. She and other moms went to PTA meetings together, participated in the local homeowner's association, and started attending ward meetings to decide upon issues to be taken to the local councilman: making sure streetlights were replaced, reporting when garbage wasn't being picked up— lots of things that tended to get neglected. The women of the street clubs had to keep reminding the local government that we were part of the city. And the church became an extension of this kind of advocacy, even from the pulpit. Mom said, "We weren't told who to vote for. We were told power was in the ballot, and if we didn't vote, we didn't have power. Everything is political. Even though we weren't told who to vote for, we were also told not to vote for people who promised not to raise taxes because taxes pay for things society needs and care for poor people. We have to have taxes, or our system won't work."

Community care and self-care—preserving ourselves—is the foundation for doing social justice work; if we are not working on our own wholeness/shalom, it will be much harder to work for wholeness on behalf of other individuals or systems. The recognition of and tending to our humanity is critical. Structures of violence and injustice operate by dehumanizing. If we remember nothing else, if we know nothing else, a first step in undoing cycles of violence is recognizing patterns of dehumanization and interrupting them. This is resistance.

3

RESILIENCE

IN AUGUST 1961, DIANE NASH, CO-FOUNDER OF THE
Student Nonviolent Coordinating Committee (SNCC) and one of
the primary organizers of the campaign to desegregate Nashville's
lunch counters, addressed the National Catholic Conference for
Interracial Justice.[1] The gathering took place a year after the
successful Nashville campaign. While Nash reflected on the
campaign, her remarks to the group also included what it had felt
like for her to experience visceral segregation everywhere she
looked when she transferred to Fisk University 1959. Originally
from Chicago, she had not experienced Jim Crow laws as blatantly.

> Seeing signs designating 'white' or 'colored,' being told,
> "We don't serve niggers in here," and, as happened in one
> restaurant, being looked in the eye and told, "Go around to
> the back door where you belong," had a tremendous psycho-

---

1. The NCCIJ was founded in 1960, just two years after the U.S. Catholic statement on racial discrimination and segregation. The Conference ended their work in
2002.

logical impact on me. To begin with, I didn't agree with the premise that I was inferior, and I had a difficult time complying with it. Also, I felt stifled and boxed in since so many areas of living were restricted. The Negro in the South is told constantly, "You can't sit here." "You can't work there." "You can't live here, or send your children to school there." "You can't use this park, or that swimming pool," and on and on and on.[2]

Nash went on to describe what she called the "curious values" Jim Crow put on the psyche of Black people who knew they were not inferior, yet were compelled to participate in the rules of a segregated society so as not to be killed. "Each time he uses a colored facility, he testifies to his own inferiority."[3]

In her talk, Nash systematically identified the cost of institutionalized oppression on Black people and its ultimate cost to all of society. She appealed to her own religious community to understand the work of resistance as the work of religion, noting that demonstrations aim to get people to pay attention and to see the evil being perpetuated and acknowledge the (willful?) ignorance of those who claimed the work has already been done, she stressed the work must continue even though the work is costly. She recounted the violence done to the student Freedom Riders and the beatings that John Lewis and others endured as they continued to show up for the cause. She told them about the angry mob of thousands who had surrounded a church in Montgomery where the Freedom Riders were holding a meeting. Martial law was declared in Montgomery that night. Nash asked, "Is this really the country in which we live?" She recalled the songs of enslaved

2. Diane Nash. "National Catholic Conference For Interracial Justice, Detroit, Michigan, August 1961" In *Women and the Civil Rights Movement, 1954-1965*, Davin W. Houck and David E. Dixon, eds. 154–68. University Press of Mississippi, 2009. http://www.jstor.org/stable/j.ctt2tvf4t.22.
3. Nash.

elders whose resistance/liberation songs figured prominently in the youth-led movement: "And before I'll be a slave, I'll be buried in my grave…"

"Is this really the country in which we live?" The question is still heartbreakingly relevant. The work of the freedom fighters continues, facing age-old threats and new ones.

Nash's reflections were also a testament to what we understand now as generational trauma. Much important work is being done to tell us about how generational trauma lives in our cells, in our DNA, and is passed down from one generation to the next. Resmaa Menakem, in *My Grandmother's Hands: Racialized Trauma and the Pathway to Mending Our Hearts and Bodies* calls this intergenerational transmission of trauma a "soul wound" that is housed in the bodies of all born and socialized in the U.S.: "white body supremacy and our adaptations to it are in our blood. Our very bodies house the unhealed dissonance and trauma of our ancestors."

I imagine the twenty-three-year-old Nash, standing before a conference of religious racial justice workers convening in the 2nd year of their organization's existence, wanting to hear the testimony of a person on the front lines of their cause. I know in my bones how necessary these gatherings are for support and encouragement, and from experience, I know the kind of pushback and backlash such gatherings are subject to. I know what it means to sit with the question "Is this my country?" and to have at least part of the response be: we cannot live like this.

Maria Yellow Horse Brave Heart defines historical trauma as a cumulative emotional and psychological wounding over a lifetime and across generations, creating a massive group trauma.[4] Unresolved grief adds to the trauma. She developed a model to understand and begin to heal from such trauma for the Lakota people,

---

4. Maria Yellow Horse Brave Heart, "Wakiksuyapi: Carrying the Historical Trauma of the Lakota." *Tulane Studies in Social Welfare* 21, no. 22 (2000): 245-266.

building on work that had been done with Holocaust survivors. This model includes facing the past by naming, remembering, and mourning it, using the power of narrative, storytelling, and remembering as an essential element of anti-oppression work. These narratives memorialize the past and equip the surviving community to build a new reality. Bearing witness to the historical harms committed against your people while experiencing the repetition of those harms in your own life compounds the impact. While the phenomenon is not new, generational trauma is not yet widely understood or appreciated. The pushback against teaching the truth of the U.S.'s racialized history and attacks on critical race theory and 'wokeness' illustrate this exceptionally well.

Lack of empathy for groups that are stereotyped and marginalized by the ruling class perpetuate and normalize the violence that is done to them. The long history of criminalizing Black people's mere existence is evidenced by specific historical situations, such as making literacy illegal and also punishing any white person who would teach an enslaved Black person to read. Any attempt to better ones' condition is impossible because it's against the law. Enslaved people did not own anything, even their bodies, so escaping was a criminal act—theft of property. Again, anyone who aided was also criminalized. White people were deputized into capturing any suspected runaway slave; even free Black people were bound under the idea that if you are walking around free, you are in the wrong.

Dr. Joy DeGruy's work focuses on the impacts of generations of oppression for Black people in the Americas. In *Post Traumatic Slave Syndrome*, DeGruy asks about the effect our history has had on our cultures and our souls.[5] She hypothesizes the trauma experience of those enslaved are a form of PTSD, using symptoms described by the *Diagnostic Statistical Manual of Mental Disorders V.* Those stressor

---

5. Joy Degruy, *Post Traumatic Slave Syndrome: America's Legacy of Enduring Injury and Healing.* (Joy DeGruy Publications, Inc, 2017), 95.

criteria include direct exposure, witnessing, or learning that a close relative or friend was exposed to death, threatened death or serious injury, or actual or threatened sexual violence OR repeated exposure to details of such events. Because enslaved people were exposed to and experienced these stressors as a "normal" part of their existence, Degruy notes a PTSD diagnosis would absolutely be appropriate.

As the condition of enslavement was passed down from mother to child, so too did the stressors and the symptoms include intrusive memories, trauma-related emotions (fear, horror, anger, guilt, shame), hypervigilance, negative beliefs and expectations about the world, and so on.

PTSD diagnoses were first recognized among soldiers and veterans; this recognition eventually led to treatment plans for them, but such resources were not available to enslaved Africans and their descendants. Dr. DeGruy and others make clear that African Americans have experienced a legacy of trauma, while others would argue "it wasn't so bad." It happened a long time ago, so get over it.

Epigenetic research of the 20th century has taught us about the changes in genetic memory—that our DNA carries the memory of the trauma experienced by our ancestors. Degruy defines Post Traumatic Slave Syndrome as "a condition that exists when a population has experienced multigenerational trauma resulting from centuries of slavery and continues to experience oppression and institutional racism today."[6] The refusal to recognize these traumas on a societal basis serves to perpetuate and deepen the trauma and its effects. Menakem's work insists that the descendants of colonizers and slaveholders carry a trauma of their own that needs to be tended to.

Genetics likely contributed to my recently diagnosed chronic health condition, hypertension, but my genetic predisposition

---

6. Degruy, 105.

(upon my mother's diagnosis at age 23, she was immediately hospitalized to ward off a stroke; my father died of a heart attack when he was 61) is not a simple tale of bad genes, bad choices or stupidity. Indeed, I've more than once had the experience of medical professionals talking to me as if I were a not-very-bright child, and/or have not taken my health concerns seriously. There is ample data and historical record documenting how attitudes and beliefs around race, gender, and class lead to poor and even deadly outcomes for patients who are of color, women, and poor. The combination of these realities complicates discerning what is actually at work here, because I do carry a bit of self-blame when I think about food choices and eating habits over the years—did I do this to myself? Can I reverse the damage that I may have done to my body with a bevy of restrictions and lifestyle changes? But growing up watching my mother struggle with her high blood pressure taught me to be careful about what I eat and how I manage the things that I am able to regarding my health. To arrive at the point where my blood pressure is unmanageable without medical intervention feels like a betrayal. So, what has this country's history of racial oppression done to alter my genes and the genes of my children? How has that history shaped what we believe about ourselves, how we treat ourselves and each other, and the kinds of stories we tell?

In *Worlds of Hurt: Reading the Literature of Trauma*, Kali Tal argues that the dominant culture politicizes traumatic experiences when those experiences are reinterpreted and appropriated to maintain the status quo.[7] Thus, the imagining of the period of enslavement that described enslaved people as childlike creatures that were happy to serve their masters while simultaneously describing Black people, especially men, as violent savages who need to be contained and controlled for the good of white society. We get the

---

7. Tal, Kali. Worlds of Hurt: Reading the Literature of Trauma. New York: Cambridge University Press, 1996, 19.

re-interpretation of the Civil Rights Movement that focuses on the content of one's character but downplays the impact of the color of one's skin. We get the persistent image of Black children not as children, but as dangerous adults.

In August of 2014, the summer Michael Brown was killed by police officer Darren Wilson, my youngest son was only a year older than the 18-year-old Brown. The week of Brown's murder I and other faculty were arriving back on campus, preparing for our fall classes. One of mine was a sociology class on race that I teach every year. While my immediate processing of Brown's death was as a Black person, and particularly as a Black mother, I also knew that I had to hold in tension my identity as a Black professor teaching at a predominantly white college.

That tension means my awareness of my identities and my lived experience; my understanding of the long history of the policing of Black bodies, extending as far back as the founding and building of this nation; and my growing awareness of the research on secondary and generational trauma coexist with whatever stories people carry about a Black woman professor teaching about peace and justice. My motives for teaching what I teach and my credentials have been challenged, sometimes by students. When I was in my Ph.D. program, there were a number of times I was told (always by a white man) how lucky I was to be a double (at least) minority, because I would easily get lots of job offers; the sub-text being, of course, that I would not actually be qualified for or obtain a position on my own merit.

In upper-level courses, students tend to self-select to be in my class because it's part of their program and they are interested in the topic. In the workshops I do outside the college, the folks I collaborate with do their best to vet participants to make sure people understand what they are signing up for, and that they have at least a baseline agreement that racism and other systems of oppression are actual problems that need solutions. Pushback is common because racism and white supremacy are deeply embedded in our history and culture and continue to be deeply misunderstood by those who insist on defining racism as individual prejudices that everyone has. Some folks come to a workshop or class because they thought it was going to be a study of multiculturalism and diversity and more "fun." Some don't believe racism exists but end up in my classes to fulfill curricular requirements (in which case they can be extra salty). These folks may tune me out or respond to me in their assignments with their own 'truths' or as has happened on occasion, shout me down in the classroom. In her essay in the book *Being Black, Teaching Black: Politics and Pedagogy in Religious Studies*, Nancy Lynn Westfield writes of the deeply embedded stereotypes of Black women that are actively in the consciousness of students "... encountering a Black woman professor is a major contradiction of terms and norms, so much that it creates for students a kind of cognitive dissonance...a Black woman with a mind and with sanctioned authority was inconceivable and unimaginable."[8] In the same text, Stephen Ray discusses how white people, in discussions of race in the academy, experience these discussions as an assault that triggers defense mechanisms on their behalf, including personal guilt and resentment.[9]

My problem as an educator in the wake of Brown's murder, and the next, and the next was that I knew I had to talk about this young boy, this mother's son who was gunned down for no good reason, his lifeless body left for hours in the street, and I did not want him to be a "lesson." I wanted to grieve. I wanted to cry and scream and rage, and mostly, I wanted to be held in the arms of the Black community so we could do those things together. I resented the fact that Brown's or any other person's death had to be the

---

8. Westfield, Nancy Lynn, Called Out My Name, or Had I Known You Were Somebody in Being Black, Teaching Black: Politics and Pedagogy in Religious Studies, Nashville: Abington Press, 2008, 67.
9. Ray, Stephen G. Jr., E-Racing While Black, in Being Black, Teaching Black: Politics and Pedagogy in Religious Studies, Nashville: Abington Press, 2008, 45.

"proof" people needed to understand and believe the destructive power of white supremacist ideology.

Yet as I resisted the notion of needing proof of the injustice done to this child and others, it was evident that Brown's death that year did seemingly pull the scales from some people's eyes, and offer "proof" that racism did exist. Even then, though, too much of the narrative was dumbed down to a "one bad apple" mythology. According to that mythology, policing (the system) was not the problem. Darren Wilson (the individual) was.

Most of the kids in my Cleveland neighborhood were raised by parents who, like mine, had migrated from the south. Many of us traveled "down home," as our parents called it, every summer to visit the relatives who still lived there. Our southern cousins would make fun of our northern accents, one of the markers of being between two ways of being in the world. Within that Black world, a notable exception also shaped me.

In 1957, my congregation's founding members envisioned a church grounded in Anabaptist/Mennonite theology but one that would not present barriers to people seeking a church community who might have assumed this community was not for them. They made the decision to not use Mennonite as part of the church name; instead, it was, from the very beginning, a "community" church that was intentionally interracial—rare during this era and still not the norm. Together, they attempted to live out the creed on a sign in the sanctuary—"One in Christ, and you are all siblings." The sign in front of the church, which I saw every Sunday growing up, read "An Equal Opportunity Faith Family." Even as the neighborhood was experiencing the last vestiges of white flight, Black and white members have continued to worship together at Lee Heights for over 50 years.

For my elders having a mixed church was not the goal. The goal was to be a visible representation of what they understood to be God's vision for humanity. It was a desire to be genuinely counter-cultural by not only offering a vague "welcome" to one another but also doing the hard work of co-existing in a larger context that actively and often violently opposed such actions. Because I continue to be part of the Christian Anabaptist community, I share this story often to help people know about my socialization as a person of faith, and how this community laid the foundation for the kind of work that has consumed me for many decades. And I also tell this story to bear witness to the hard work and the long-term commitment necessary to sustain such a vision. In the model of antiracism training that I do, truth-telling by recounting a history of structural racism in the US is a foundation. We must begin our work by naming how U.S. institutions came into being when the land mass that would become the U.S. was blatantly and unapologetically structured around the notion of white supremacy. It is an ugly history, and while it is not the only history, it is what must be faced.

Bearing witness to this history requires accountability: What shall we do now that we know about our historical context and what we have inherited? How do we hold ourselves accountable for creating new systems and structures that do not uphold the notion that humanity exists along a hierarchy? The question remains: Who gets to be seen, whose stories are heard, and whose stories are valued?

Resilience comes from living into the answers to these questions: Who are your people? Who are the ones who brought you into being, nurtured you, and taught you who you are? This could refer to literal family bloodlines, but I use the word family expansively here. When I think about the people who brought me into being, it's my family, but it's also the neighborhood I grew up in and the faith community that nurtured me. It's the books that I read and how I was nurtured by the people who wrote these books—my early foray into Black feminist essays, essays and poems and stories written by queer people, and other people who were consciously in women-centered communities. It's the writers of the Harlem Renaissance. It's womanist theologians and ethicists. All these and more are people who brought me into being.

Our people are the ones who call us into who we are, the ones who paved the way so that we could be here. Our people are aligned with the work we want to do in the world, and this, too, is expansive. We don't do our best work in silos. We certainly don't do movement work when we only have a very narrow vision of what that work encompasses; part of the answer to this question depends on understanding the big picture and the long arc of the movement work. What is the historical context? Who were the heroes, speakers, and movers of the past? What did they have to overcome to get where they did, no matter how little or long that journey was? One of the reasons that I love to peel back and look at historical context when teaching my students about systemic oppression is because it shows with that broad view how many people were involved, how long the campaigns were, and where the people came from to get together. The college students who were engaged in desegregating lunch counters in the 1960s spent their summers doing freedom rides and sit-ins, knowing what the cost was going to be. They learned that much of what they were doing would cause pain but also advance the cause. The knowledge that they were not alone indeed kept them going.

Movements need many bodies, minds, and spirits that can contribute in various ways, many unseen. Who made resources available for the work for the lunch counter protests, the Freedom Rides, the Black Lives Matter protests, or any mass movement? How do people get back and forth from home to work to a protest at the voting booth? The Montgomery Bus Boycott lasted over 300 days, and people still had to get to work. Some had their jobs threatened for participating. Livelihoods and safety were at risk because they dared to speak out for liberty, freedom, and equality. Churches and other community buildings made their spaces available after hours; dozens of people cooked meals so that folks could gather and organize and prepare after having worked all day. Black taxi drivers reduced their fares. Who are the people who support your work?

How do we interact with those who oppose us? And what do we need to do to support those living lives that are constrained due to work, family, health/disability/mobility issues? Who has access to being a part of this movement? Who's getting the information out there? Who's organizing people so that new folks are constantly joining this river of folks doing the work? And who brings their innovation, ideas, energy, and blood? How do we honor, respect, and work with each other across lines of difference that are used to pit us against one another, for instance, generational lines?

Each semester, students in my conflict class read Allen Johnson's *Privilege, Power, and Difference*, first published in 2001. They read independently, and then, twice during the semester, they discuss the book in small groups. One semester, a group expressed surprise that someone of Johnson's generation (he was born in 1946) was talking about race and racism, as if their generation was the first to do so. In that same semester, a student in another class wrote in a reflection paper that the names and places of people we were discussing were new to them; their education before college had never had content about race. Our movements will have people entering them from many different backgrounds and journeys. We must avoid hubris about our group of people and understand that generational tendencies are just that: tendencies and generalizations. They are not a magical formula that tells us who everyone is and how they will act in every circumstance.

Recently, I gave a talk about long-term anti-racism work at another college, in which I discussed the importance of resilience and creative strategies. In the Q&A afterward, someone asked about the importance of resilience because Black youth are often told by their elders—parents, guardians, teachers, and others—that they have to work twice as hard to get half as far as their white counterparts. This is something that I heard from adults when I was growing up, and I know that my elders heard it from the generations above them. There is a truth to this. It is pragmatic but also a deflating reality. The grit narrative is real—I've had so many discussions about the need to prove that we are hard workers and that we are worthy of the opportunities we have been given. I'm also grateful that more and more people are looking at that narrative and saying "I'm not gonna do that." In light of what we are fighting for, we cannot perpetuate unhealthy life-work balances (in the places we can choose not to do so—this is not true for everyone!) to get our work done. Liberation also means rethinking what success is and what it looks like. For Black people and other people of color, it means balancing a healthy relationship with work, and the narrative that says that we are lazy drains on society because we need to consider what we pass on. What do we tell our Black and Brown children who are growing up in a world that demonstrates over and over and over again that it does not love them, does not care for them, and does not want them to succeed? It doesn't even want them to be around unless it is to entertain. Do sports, sing, and dance. Entertain us, yes, but other than that, keep quiet and stay out of the way. Driving back to Indiana after the talk, seeing multiple Confederate flags and other symbols provided evidence of people's disdain for folks who look like me and do the work I do. I suspect if I were to engage one of those flag flyers or people who have anti-BLM or other progressive movements on their cars, they would probably tell me no, this doesn't mean that I hate you. This means that I stand for "American values."

My plan is to be engaged in this struggle for the rest of my life; therefore I need restorative practices to replenish what the work takes from me emotionally, spiritually, and physically. If I want to invite others to join me, it will help if my life is not in a shambles because of self-neglect in those areas. While social-emotional learning is under attack and critical race theory debates rage, self-care is crucial.

Though some argue we should shield children from society's

painful history, marginalized youth already live with daily oppression. Adults addressing injustice must model balancing hard truths with compassion for our shared humanity. It has been said that those who want to wage peace must prepare as diligently as those who prepare for war. For me, part of that is building appropriate resilience strategies into my teaching, beginning with building in the expectation that we would develop the capacity to talk about hard things.

I wrote a statement that we read together in the first week of class. Each person has their own copy, and we read the document aloud, each taking a couple of sentences. (Passes are allowed for those who prefer not to read aloud.) In essence, the document asserts the desire for our classroom and community to be as safe a space as we can make it.

It reads:

> While recognizing that safe space cannot be guaranteed, what we can do is commit ourselves to crafting a safer space.

> As the instructor for this course, I commit myself to not doing violence by my words or by my deeds. If and when I make mistakes I ask that it be brought to my attention. I will do my best to make it right.

> As participants, I ask that you do the same: to commit yourselves to not doing violence by word or by deed.

> Let us together recognize that all of us are on a journey, and we are at different places on the journey.

> We recognize that we come from a number of different spaces and places, and have different lived experiences.

We recognize that as we gather together for this class we come from a spectrum of theological, political, social and economic perspectives and commitments.

There are probably many points in which we do not agree with one another. But we would like to hold all of who we are and what we bring together in this place in a community of mutual discernment and caring for one another.

The study of conflict, violence, and trauma is hard work, emotionally and psychologically. All of the participants in the course are asked to commit to practicing self and community care. I call this radical self-care, and that notion is drawn from the Audre Lorde quote at the top of the page.[10]

Self-care is part of the foundation for social justice work; if we are working on our own wholeness (shalom), it will be easier to work for wholeness on behalf of other individuals or systems. The recognition of and tending to our own humanity is critical.

Structures of violence and injustice operate by dehumanizing. Therefore, a first step in undoing cycles of violence is recognizing patterns of dehumanization and interrupting them.

In this course, committing ourselves to radical self and community care involves the following (at the very least):

- Identifying and committing to self-care practices

10. "Caring for myself is not self-indulgence. It is self-preservation, and that is an act of political warfare."

regularly, and regularly reporting on your practices. You will get credit for this, but please note – this is not something you can skip and then make up at the end of the semester – this defeats the entire purpose of the assignment!

- Participate in small group discussions to process class content (getting out of our heads)
- Assume leadership at least once during the semester for community care
- Thoughtful response to/discussion with peers when research is presented

I started including this disclaimer and focus for our work at the beginning of the semester in this class because I saw students struggling to handle the course content and all the other things they needed to tend to as people with complicated, busy lives. The "easiest" thing for some of them to do would be to avoid class or not to do the readings. Of course, this defeated the purpose of taking the class. It also took away from how I envisioned us processing the information as a community, mainly supporting each other's research.

While I and other professors do what we can in our spaces, it's also vital that our institutions support that work. In the current climate, this is increasingly difficult work, and we must look to the strategies of our forebears to determine how to do what we must do. This is much easier said than done on some campuses than on others. While I recognize that leaders of institutions have many lines of accountability to which they are held, I also long for the kind of boldness and risk-taking that anti-oppression work requires.

For many people, the summer of 2020 was like something out of a dystopian novel. As the reality of the global pandemic set in, the world's attention was also riveted on a series of discrete but connected events concerning Black people's body autonomy and right to exist and state-sponsored violence. At the end of May, cities across the nation and the globe erupted into protests. We came back to our campuses apprehensive and unsure of what the future held for our teaching in what was once again an opportunity to go forward or retreat. We came back changed because of the pandemic and what it meant for the way education happens. In the midst of it all, we had an opportunity to talk about race and face the problems of racism in our communities and on our campuses.

Historically, too many institutions have fallen into the trap of understanding racism as singular, interpersonal problems that are solved by teaching people to "be better." That insistence on the interpersonal nature of racism has hampered our ability for institutions and society at large to critically examine their policies, procedures, and practices. This lack of foundation aids in what we are currently observing in the rapid-fire dismantling of human and civil rights gains over the last century. Facing this country's long history of racial segregation and how it affects who we know and how we know them is also necessary. A 2014 Public Religion Research Institute study revealed that most white people have at most, one Black friend.[11] The study carefully drew distinctions between friends (someone with whom you regularly discuss important issues, not just things related to work, someone who has visited your home and you've visited theirs, etc.) and acquaintances. Many of our students (white and of color) remark that coming to college has given them the most diverse experience yet of their young lives. To be clear, it's not that friendship is the magic pill, but deliberate policies that separate those deemed "other" have a cumulative and destructive social cost at every level.

Ignorance about the history of systemic racism hampers any institution's ability to face up to the racial conditions of the

11. Christopher Ingraham, "Three quarters of whites don't have any non-white friends," The Washington Post, August 25, 2014, https://www.washingtonpost.com/news/wonk/wp/2014/08/25/three-quarters-of-whites-dont-have-any-non-white-friends/?wpmm=AG0003386.

current era. If we don't know, or forget, that most educational institutions denied access to African Americans (and other people of color and women) in their histories, it's pretty easy to assume there are other reasons why the schools remain primarily white. We have witnessed how these narratives become a truth, and any remedies applied are attempts to "fix" the person and not the institutions. Our educational systems should recognize that such remedial approaches toward students are not enough. Instead, the forces of white supremacy regularly demand erasure of and retreat from this knowledge. Sometimes (especially after a violent event), institutions provide opportunities for people to learn. However, in education, this often focuses solely on students, leading to situations where the students are more competent in discussing race than the faculty and staff and, more importantly, where faculty and staff are held to a different level of accountability than students. This explains in part why some of my students were so surprised that a white person of Allen Johnson's generation willingly and competently wrote about racism and other systemic violences.

In times of crisis and in their quieter aftermaths, our institutions need to hold their agents accountable for building racial and cultural competency skills, unlearning stereotypes, and becoming aware of conscious and unconscious biases. Competency in these areas means more than knowing what words to say and not say. People need competency in interrupting the narrative, which means knowing what the narrative is and how we have been compelled to be complicit with it. Students from groups that have been minoritized and stigmatized are painfully aware of their simultaneous hypervisibility and invisibility. For example, a frequent assumption about Black students is that they attend college to play a sport and that they are unprepared for academics. This is true for some Black students; it is also true for some white students and other students of color. The over-association of Black students (and Black people in general) with sports and other forms of entertainment reflects the avenues that have been allowed for Black people to achieve prominence.

Employees and board members should be held accountable for learning anti-oppression practices. When it's optional (so often the case), learning opportunities are attended by the same small group, likely with the least institutional power to make any changes. The status quo is not questioned. Leaning into anti-racist practices would mean that institutions are watching for and tending to staff of color who take on formal and informal mentoring of new people of color in the community. In higher ed, faculty of color are instrumental in helping students of color navigate predominantly white campuses. They might be seeking assurance that they made the right choice in choosing their school, looking for resources (like where to get a haircut), or simply finding comfort in faces that look like theirs. However, their concerns are not limited to adjusting to college life and navigating their new academic home. Students are also processing the trauma brought about by witnessing (through video replays on social media) and hearing about the killings of Black people. Hearing comments about how the victims were responsible for their deaths is re-traumatizing. Black faculty and staff, who are processing their own grief and fear, are often the first persons on campus that affected students reach out to.

Faith-based organizations are often confused about the best way to do the work of anti-racism. Context matters—the make-up of staff, the constituencies to whom the institution holds itself accountable, and the lived experiences of marginalized bodies within the institution. However, there are some typical "to-dos" including renewing the emphasis on intercultural dialogue, with anti-racism education and organizing as part of its continued witness to the theological commitments of the community. To do so, institutions must equip their leaders and members to speak not only about Black lives but about white rage and fear that fuels the attacks mentioned earlier on Black bodies. Their anti-racism work must build recognition that racism and ensuing violence are structural and institution-alized, and to address this, the denomination must speak to and with its structures and institutions. This would further mean that agencies, educational institutions, and conferences affiliated with the denominational body commit resources to continued anti-oppression education among its constituencies. This commitment includes acknowledging how the denomination's institutions have been complicit and silent in the face of growing anti-Black bias. Additionally, the denomination can offer resources to aid in the healing and renewal of communities that have experienced violence because of individual racial hatred AND institutionalized racism. It can stand in solidarity with communities that are speaking out against police brutality and offer material aid and personnel (at the invitation of affected communities) to rebuild destroyed properties.

Faith-based institutions seek to diversify their staff and leader-ship and to be equipped for an increasingly diverse, troubled, and violent U.S. society in the twenty-first century. Although some still insist that we live in a post-racial world, highly publicized acts of violence against Black bodies and other bodies of color are regu-larly featured in mainstream media and on social media. White society and churches, predominantly white churches, are again being asked to speak up and hold themselves accountable to marginalized people. They are being challenged not to let white Christianity be defined by racism, fear, and xenophobia. They are being challenged to do what the Radical Reformers did—speak out against the empire even at the peril of losing their comfort within it. This means also taking actions outside the church and supporting policies that value Black lives—for instance, educating about and working to tear down the prison-industrial complex.

These institutions can formalize curricula to educate about the racialized history of the United States. History and theology classes can further articulate how this history has impacted how mission and service work has been and continues to be done. Mission boards can take steps to decolonize their work.

Multiple diverse voices must be part of the organizing strategy. It is critically essential for white people to talk about white supremacy and racism; in the same way, men must speak about sexism, and straight people must talk about heterosexism. Those with more social power can take advantage of their placement in the hierarchy and use it to dismantle it. While this best happens in the community context, it must also be under the leadership of those with marginalized identities. Marginalized people know best what white supremacy/sexism/heterosexism is doing to them and understand it as a matter of urgency. It is life or death.

That visit my family made to the Smithsonian Museum of African American History and Culture brought up complex reckonings with the legacy of our Christian faith tradition. Seeing the evidence of Christianity's complicity in the slave trade and perpetuating enslavement once again confronted me with brutal truths. I see how so many enduring Black church traditions carried remnants of ancestral practices that were outlawed and deemed evil or demonic.

Our resistance needs resilience. The part of the work for change that we may miss, especially in a context where the expectation for so many things is instant gratification, is the need to build up the capacity to stay in the struggle for justice for a long time, to know what your role is, and to be in community—because we were never meant to do this work alone.

Writer, historian, and activist Rebecca Solnit writes in *Hope in the Dark: Untold Histories: Wild Possibilities*:

Cause and effect assume history marches forward, but history is not an army. It is a crab scuttling sideways, a drop of soft water wearing away stone, an earthquake breaking centuries of tension. Sometimes one person inspires movement, or her words do decades later, sometimes a few passionate people change the world, sometimes they start a mass movement, and millions do, sometimes those millions are stirred by the same outrage or the same idea, and change comes upon us like a change of weather. All that these transformations have in common is that they begin in the imagination, in hope. To hope is to gamble. It's to bet on the future, on your desires, on the possibility that an open heart and uncertainty is better than gloom and safety. To hope is dangerous, and yet it is the opposite of fear, for to live is to risk.[12]

She goes on to say that action is impossible without hope. I continue to cling to hope, and I need others to cling with me.

In the epilogue of *Sisters in the Wilderness*, theologian Delores Williams noted the resilience and resistance capacities of the biblical Hagar and Black women in America. According to Williams, survival strategies that kept hope alive in Black communities included cunning, the art of encounter, and the arts of care and connection. The art of cunning is knowledge combined with skill and dexterity, using imagination and skill that fostered the economic well-being of the Black family. Resistance and endurance are movements in the art of encounter—acting at the right time is part of an overall strategy—not an accident.[13]

---

12. Solnit, Rebecca. *Hope in the Dark: Untold Histories, Wild Possibilities*. Chicago, Haymarket Books. 2016, 4.
13. Williams, Delores. *Sisters in the Wilderness*, 236.

4

RADICAL LOVE

I DON'T REMEMBER THE FIRST TIME I GOT MY HAIR straightened with a hot comb, heated on the stove old-school style. I do remember that, at some point, I started going across the street to Mrs. White's house every Saturday morning so that she could press my hair. It was undoubtedly a Black girl's rite of passage at the time, graduating from wearing kinky, coily, little girl braids to pressed hair that one couldn't get wet, or the hair would revert to its natural state. Getting my hair pressed felt normal. I wouldn't say I liked the process, but I didn't hate the result because most of the Black women and girls I knew got their hair straightened. And while it was rare to see Black people on television, most of them also had pressed hair. But while I was a child, there was a movement going on that was about more than civil rights—the Black is Beautiful movement. The afro–Black people's hair was symbolic of that movement, which was left in its natural state, free and unencumbered. When I was twelve, there was a barber shop I passed every day on the way home from school. One day, I ducked in, got my hair cut, and emerged later with an afro of my own. My mother was shocked but gave me the beautiful gift of body autonomy. In this small way, she reflected a larger movement that Blackness was not ugly, bad, or wrong despite all of the cultural, political, and religious messages that said that it was.

The Black is Beautiful movement was built on the struggle for Black liberation. The phrase took back the narrative that blackness was negative, ugly, something not to be desired. Part of its foundation was the Black Arts movement. These movements are integral to the ways Black people created, re-created, and celebrated Blackness and Black culture in a society that did not value us. Loving Blackness, despite what the surrounding culture says about Black people and Black culture, continues to be a necessary fuel to all Black liberation movements. Legislation that orchestrated Black people's lives from birth to the grave (literally, because hospitals, cemeteries, and everything in between were segregated) was meant in large part to socialize generation after generation into America's racial hierarchy. The hierarchy, in turn, socialized negative thinking and behavior toward Black people, even within the Black community. Within the racial hierarchy, proximity to whiteness (like straight hair and light skin) was more valued and could result in tangible benefits like employment, housing, and education. The Black Arts Movement refuted the notion of Black inferiority while detailing how the idea of white supremacy sought to keep the hierarchy in place. In her poem, *Primer for Black* Gwendolyn Brooks turns the "one-drop" rule on its head. Its original intent was to ensure lower status on anyone with a hint of Black ancestry. Brooks proclaims:

The word Black
has geographic power,
pulls everybody in:
Blacks here—
Blacks there—
Blacks wherever they may be.
And remember, you Blacks, what they told you—

remember your Education:
"one Drop—one Drop
maketh a brand new Black."
Oh mighty Drop.
_____And because they have given us kindly
so many more of our people
Blackness
stretches over the land.
Blackness—
the Black of it,
the rust-red of it,
the milk and cream of it,
the tan and yellow-tan of it,
the deep-brown middle-brown high-brown of it,
the "olive" and ochre of it—
Blackness
marches on.[1]

The geographic power Brooks speaks of highlights the historic preoccupation of white people with the ancestry/humanity of Black people in the U.S.—the one-drop rule that designated anyone with "one drop" (read: any ancestry) of Black blood as Black, not for simple demographic accounting, but to know how that person should be treated in a society that segregated and denied rights to people based on race. However, geographic power works both ways and overpowers the diminishing or destroying forces. Blackness marches on and creates a new reality.

Justice work is ultimately a declaration of love. It's not the Hallmark card notion of romantic love or a devotion to the latest obsessive trend. When we love authentically, we do not know what the journey's outcome will be—we hope we know where this thing is going, but make the choice without assurances. If we are honest,

---

1. Gwendolyn Brooks, *Primer for Blacks*, Chicago: Third World Press, 1991, 9.

we know there will be disappointments, setbacks, and downright hard times. Our loved ones—family, friends, lovers—are imperfect and fallible. To enter into love means taking a risk to join our stories, hearts, minds, and futures without knowing where the journey will take us, but committed to doing our part the best we can, moment by moment. The work of social change is done with a vision of the world we want to see, but no promise that we will see the fulfillment of that vision through our contributions. We move by faith in our vision of justice, and if we are wise, build on the work done by the folks who came before us, assess our gifts and capabilities, and strategize with others to the best of our abilities. We recognize our connectedness and interdependence with one another; we realize the beauty and strength we embody as individuals and communities. And we care for all of this with tenderness and joy. As bell hooks noted, "Without an ethic of love shaping the direction of our political vision and our radical aspirations, we are often seduced, in one way or the other, into continued allegiance to systems of domination—imperialism, sexism, racism, classism."[2]

Systems of domination are seductive, and consciously so. Goading people into setting up systems of winners and losers, of good people (like us) and enemies, nurtures discontent and competition under the illusion that the playing field is equal. Work hard enough and squash the "other" successfully enough; the promise is that you will come out on top. Systems of domination depend on hate, fear, suspicion, and hatred. It works well when people with marginalized identities get sucked into the game and even better when the hate, fear, and suspicion are turned on us and those who look like us or are members of other marginalized groups. This keeps attention away from the destructive systems that depend upon marginalized communities to be pitted against each other and not to notice the complex web of identities that

---

2. bell hooks, "Love as the Practice of Freedom" in *Outlaw Culture: Resisting Representations*, (New York: Routledge, 1994), 289.

make us who we are. In decades past and even present, it can be frighteningly easy to germinate and nurture friction between groups as though people do not belong to more than one group at a time. If Central American immigrants, U.S.-born Black people, and trans people of any race/ethnicity are fighting with and against each other, none of us gets free. Sometimes, there is no animosity towards another group, but we have been taught that aligning ourselves with certain groups means withdrawing support from the systems of power. One of the most essential things marginalized groups can do is to understand how our struggles are connected. We must show up for ourselves and each other in our commonalities and how we are different from one another. It takes a vision and a will to do the seed planting and tending. It means being prepared for disagreement and conflict. It can be counterintuitive.

The exhilaration of being with "our people" is magical. It is that rare space that we sometimes have to claw our way into, and when we get there and find it when we find our people, it is precious. The danger of protecting that space so carefully is that it can become like the oppressive spaces we were fleeing. We may not notice it, but others will. We cannot do our best work in creating a world where everyone is free if we do not acknowledge how we belong to each other and how we are familiar with the valley of the shadow of death.

I cling to the belief that a force for good exists. Some know this force as God; this is part of the language of faith I was taught, and while I still use this language, my thinking is more expansive and inclusive of what I believe provides the foundation for many religious paths—we are connected, to the rest of the created order, and to the holy. The Holy One's vision for the world is shalom. We are meant to care for one another, to understand that pain, suffering, and evil persist not at the whim of a capricious deity but as a result of human choices and will and can be addressed by human decisions and will. This is not only the work of religious people but also all of our work. I don't have all of the answers to the why of suffering, and I struggle with the dogged persistence of violence and oppression. I have struggled with Christianity and with religion, mainly because religious systems have been and continue to be used to promote and justify violence. At the end of the day, I am still a person of faith, and I still believe in pursuing justice, goodness, and shalom.

Years ago, when I was a pastor and a seminary student, I asked one of my professors (who had also been a pastor), "How are we to do this, this preaching, week after week? How do we keep it fresh when so many have heard it all? How do we grab people's attention again and again?" My professor said, "You tell the story." I don't think it is a mistake that so many religious traditions have an ethic of care as a foundation. They tell us:

- Do what is right.
- Do what is fair.
- Repair the broken.
- Keep showing up.

This ethic is embedded in our narratives, which help us re-orient the world. When we tell our stories, whether they are faith narratives unfolding in scripture, the stories of our culture and our people, the re-telling of history from the perspective of the marginalized, our stories are a re-membering. They pull us back to ourselves, our calling, each other, and the Holy. They serve to ground us in what is accurate, authentic, and right. Amid the chaos, amid real fear and terror, we are asked to keep showing up. We are asked to keep telling the story.

Part of the wisdom of religious communities is the regular coming together to create a story and a history together. This is more than just showing up to check something off the list. It's more than going through the motions. When we gather—each week, each month, each liturgical season—we build the capacity to show up and respond.

For several months in 2015, the lock screen on my phone was a picture of a little African American girl in a pink dress and pink shoes standing at the door of a church. It was the Mother Emanuel AME Church in Charleston, South Carolina, where, on a Wednesday night, ten people, including the pastor, gathered for prayer and Bible Study as they did every week. On that night, a young white supremacist entered the church and subsequently opened fire on them all, killing nine people.

In the picture, an elderly dark-skinned Black man with a deeply lined face is holding the door open for the child in the pink dress. He is tall and slim, and he wears a dark jacket. On his hands are snow-white gloves that indicate his role as an usher, like in many African American churches. He is the one who welcomes people in, helps them find a seat, and helps you find your place. The photo was taken the Sunday after the murders in the church; I found it online in one of the many stories following the tragedy. I was struck by the image of him holding the door for the tiny girl standing at the threshold of the sanctuary, the gathering place for God's people, and the look on his face says, "We're still here. *We still show up*. Come on in."

There is no other way but to keep telling the story, whether for the first time, or the hundredth, or the ten thousandth time. We orient and reorient ourselves along the arc of the universe that is ever so long but that bends, even now, towards justice.[3]

Many of us have been taught to understand religion as a life-long "get into heaven" test. The prize for living right is getting to go to heaven, and too bad for the poor suckers that didn't get it right—they will be left behind. What if, instead, we understand

---

3. This sentiment, famously quoted by and often attributed to Martin Luther King, Jr., was originally said by 19th century Unitarian minister and abolitionist Rev. Theodore Parker.

our texts and the purpose for our communities as invitations to cooperation so that we all win, so that none of us is snatched away unawares and none of us is left behind?

I am committed to non-violent resistance and the directive from my faith to love one's enemies. More and more, I am finding it is a day-by-day, even moment-by-moment choice. In 2017, after the white supremacist "Unite the Right" rally in Charlottesville, David Swartz wrote a piece that describes the work clergy did to respond. Swartz highlighted the work of Christian Peacemaker Teams (now Community Peacemaker Teams), launched in the 1980s as a way for folks to prepare for peace as vigorously as those who prepare for war. Swartz illustrated four ways in which what he identified as Mennonite peacemaking played out in Charlottesville: courageous action in the face of evil, specialized techniques, a strong faith, and loving one's enemy.

Under his fourth point, Swartz quotes pastor Hillary Watson: "We have to peel back the violent and abusive parts of white supremacy until we find what the scared humans underneath are digging for: reassurance that they won't be left behind, that they have an economic future... and so on."[4] Watson discusses the ineffectiveness of meeting violence with violence and the new difficulties presented by a more boldly racist context in America. She argues for the need for pacifists to speak up in this moment, which I heartily agree with. Swartz then asserts, "Peacemakers must do the hard work of building exit ramps from white supremacy for even the most unlovable."

While those building ramps are necessary, this is specific work for specific people and not what I am called to do. Everyone can't do everything. Peacemaking in a violence-saturated world must include formation, gifts, discernment, and accountability. These are

---

4. Hillary Watson. "Before You Punch a Nazi: A New Anabaptist Response to White Supremacy." *Anabaptist World* (blog) August 15, 2017. https://anabaptist world.org/before-you-punch-a-nazi-a-new-anabaptist-response-to-white-supremacy/

very churchy words but useful and easily re-framed for any context that gathers people around a specific vision and mission.

FORMATION

If we want to be people willing to risk everything for a call to radical love and justice, we must be trained in a culture of love and justice, steeped in its practices from day to day. What in each of us is willing to be called out, nurtured, and fed so that we can all show up for the tasks to which we have been called?

GIFTS DISCERNMENT

Everything ain't for everybody. There is so much work to be done that we don't have the time to put ourselves down or feel bad that we were not on the front lines in Virginia or Charleston or any of the places violence rears its head—unless we feel within our spirit and have been told by others who see in us what we don't know that we were supposed to be there. Instead, can we not call out the gifts we see in ourselves and others and identify where they can be used in this new era?

ACCOUNTABILITY

What are we willing to ask of each other in this task of justice building? Can we pay attention to how marginalized groups are often pitted against one another? Can we build ways to identify that and resist it? Can we honestly say to one another, I've got your back"? Can we practice loving our enemies by loving our non-enemies a bit better?

Swartz' piece ends on a frustrating note for me when he cites an interaction described in an article[5] reporting on religious lead-

---

5. Jack Jenkins. "Meet the clergy who stared down white supremacists in Char-

ers' counter protest of the Unite the Right rally. In both articles, the encounter between Lisa Sharon Harper, a Black activist and writer, and one of the white protesters serves as a coda:

> Militia members were told by their leaders not to speak to protestors. But Harper, a black woman, wore down one white supremacist with words of love. As violence all around began to end their conversation, Harper told him, "I just want you to know, we love you." The man's face, grizzled and tired from the day, suddenly softened. After a moment, he replied, "I love you too."[6]

The placement of the encounter makes a nice, neat ending to an account of the power of nonviolent action. I don't object to its inclusion in the reporting—we need these stories; we need to know about people who are mobilized to stand up against hate. I'm dissatisfied because I want to know what happened next, and I suspect what this story ultimately leaves us with. It leaves us with *hope*. I sure *hope* that guy saw the errors of his ways, denounced white supremacy, and took everyone with him. I *hope* he fights as hard as Harper does to live. Maybe I'm cynical and jaded, but I don't think that's what is likely to happen. More likely, he will leave that moment and go back to a movement that tells him his manhood, his personhood, is tied up in keeping people of color and other marginalized folks down by any means necessary.

I could be wrong. But if I'm not, what does love look like in this circumstance? What does love look like for me, for you, and any of us in our homes, neighborhoods, or sanctuaries when, on any given Sunday, we don't know who among us is safe? How do we

---

lottesville." *Think Progress* (blog). August 16, 2017. https://archive.thinkprogress. org/clergy-in-charlottesville-e95752415c3e/

6. David Swartz. "A Highly Trained Nonviolent Peacekeeping Force." *Anxious Bench* (blog) *Patheos.com*, August 30, 2017. https://www.patheos.com/blogs/anxious bench/2017/08/mennonites-behind-clergy-protests-charlottesville/

live with each other? Part of the answer is that we can't wait for a catastrophe. What would an ethic of love look like if it showed up at the root of what goes into shaping the people who gather to shout, "Blood and soil" and "You will not replace us"?

I have discovered a bit of the answer, for me. Every August for the last five years has been hard because I think, "How do I teach what I teach in the aftermath of whatever the summer has wrought when we haven't recovered from whatever happened the year before?" Somehow, when speaking to people, I need to believe that peace is possible and justice is possible; I believe it again, too.

This is why we tell the story. This is why we acculturate ourselves in this community—we come to speak and hear these narratives repeatedly. To hear what the prophets say about love. We gather to say to ourselves and each other because we believe the universe is indeed ordered around this call to love and justice.

One of my elders in the Black Liberation struggle, Ruby Sales, has spoken widely on this idea of love. Sales is the founder and director of the Spirit House Project in Atlanta and spoke with podcast host Krista Tippett in an episode titled "Where does it hurt?"

Ruby is one of the wise ones. In the podcast, she talks about the grounding of Black folk religion and what it means to have people speak wholeness into you by telling you that you are loved, valuable, and beloved. Tippett asks: "How do we, with one breath and in one heart that is trying to be whole, acknowledge this rage and outrage and suffering, which is real, among so many people out on the margins of the power structures and this desire for a healing and transformative love that can lead to a beloved community?"

Ruby responded:

Well, first of all, as you just pointed out, love is not antithetical to being outraged. Let's be very clear about that. And love is not antithetical to anger. There are two kinds of anger. There's redemptive anger, and there's non-redemptive anger. And so redemptive anger is the anger that says that—that moves you to transformation and human up-building. Non-redemptive anger is the anger that white supremacy roots itself in. So, we have to make a distinction. So, people think that anger is a destructive emotion, and it's where you begin your conversation.

I became involved in the Southern Freedom Movement, not merely because I was angry about injustice, but because I love the idea of justice. So, it's where you begin your conversation. So, most people begin their conversation with "I hate this"—but they never talk about what it is they love. And so, I think that we have to begin to have a conversation that incorporates a vision of love with a vision of outrage.[7]

Beginning with the idea of love and exercising the practices of love happens in the day-to-day encounters of our relationships and builds up the muscle needed to withstand the hard work of pursuing justice. We don't wait for the feeling; we do the actions. This is the basis of what has come to be called restorative justice practices. While scholars and many practitioners trace the modern restorative justice movement to the late 1970s, its roots are within the ways that many human communities have organized themselves to deal with ruptures in the social fabric. Restorative practices assume the dignity and worth of each person and aim to listen and attend to the needs of those harmed by the actions of others. Those who commit harm are held accountable not only to the individuals who may have been harmed but to the community at large. Restorative practices place a responsibility on the community to help each other see and be seen, creating spaces where all

---

7. Ruby Sales, "Where Does it Hurt?" Interview with Krista Tippett, *On Being*, podcast audio, September 15, 2015, https://onbeing.org/programs/ruby-sales-where-does-it-hurt/.

voices can be heard. It's easy to see how more industrialized, individualized, and capitalistic societies have been separated from these ways of being, but we are continually reminded of them and called back. I love reading the wisdom of Audre Lorde for myself and my students as such reminders.

> Your silences will not protect you.... What are the words you do not yet have? What are the tyrannies you swallow day by day and attempt to make your own, until you will sicken and die of them, still in silence? We have been socialized to respect fear more than our own need for language.
>
> ... ask: What's the worst that will happen? Then push yourself a little further than you dare. Once you start to speak, people will yell at you. They will interrupt you, put you down, and suggest it's personal. And the world won't end
>
> ... And at last, you'll know with surpassing certainty that only one thing is more frightening than speaking your truth. And that is not speaking.[8]

Almost ten years ago, after the killing of yet another unarmed Black man, I wrote a piece about how a misty-eyed, overromanticized definition of love is not what we need to get us where we want to go in terms of building a world where all of us, especially the most marginalized and maligned, can not just survive, but can flourish. I'll end this book with that piece and invite any and all to join the work in whatever capacity you have at this moment. Let us love authentically and build the world we want to see.

---

8. Audre Lorde, "The Transformation of Silence into Language and Action" in *Sister Outsider: Essays and Speeches*, Berkeley: The Crossing Press, 1984, 41.

I CANNOT SPEAK OF LOVE TO YOU TODAY (JULY 2016)

Earlier this summer, my 20-year-old son had a burned-out headlight on his car. I don't know how long it had been out, but as soon as I learned about it, I was all about getting it fixed right away. We made an event of looking up the right size lamp for his vehicle, going to the auto parts store, and then going to YouTube to figure out how to do the replacement. We were successful—chalk one up for feeling accomplished and a little mother-son bonding. But frankly, I wanted to get that light changed as soon as possible because a burned-out light can be a death sentence for a Black man.

The world woke up to this truth on Wednesday morning as we learned the news of the death of Philando Castile. You likely know the details. Castile was stopped because he had a broken taillight. He was shot as he reached into his back pocket for his identification. His fiancée and her 4-year-old child were in the car and witnessed the shooting.

A few weeks ago, I had a conversation with a perfectly nice and well-meaning young white man. He explained to me how much easier it was for him to understand racism and be motivated to work against it after having developed a friendship with neighbors who are people of color. The young white man explained that this friendship helped him understand and care more about racism. The love and affection he and his family had for their neighbors—the meals and the stories they shared—had done far more than any anti-racism training or other educational piece had done. He was making the argument that, absent of personal relationships, we cannot advance the fight against racist oppression.

I used to believe this, too. When I started antiracism work, I leaned heavily on the power of personal relationships. I still believe in their power. I believe in the power of love. I believe that I am called to love.

However, the systemic nature of oppression means that oppression functions despite the goodwill, intentions, and, yes, the love of many, many people. And at the end of the day, I am more interested in my son coming home alive than I am in someone learning to love him. I said as much to the young man. I affirmed his friendship with his neighbors and tried to convey with my words that I did not belittle the transformative power of that relationship. But in 2016 America, if I have to choose between being loved and being treated with justice, I'm going to choose justice.

If my son gets stopped for a traffic violation, I can't hope that the officer who stops him loves someone who looks like him. I can and do know that the public at large—not just police officers but educators, employers, and people just walking down the street— has been socialized to view my Black son as a threat, as a criminal.

I recognize that my words limit "love" to a feeling and that the biblical command to love is much more profound than a feeling. This reflects my belief that the willingness to love across the boundaries of difference and the weight of history has not sufficiently met the biblical command. Can you affirm my humanity and right to exist without loving me, that is, having warm feelings about me? What if I'm not lovable that day? Do you get to mistreat me then? Do I have to prove my loveability—my worthiness of your love—over and over and over again? Or do I just get to be? These are serious questions.

At a traffic stop for a burned-out headlight, I can't gamble on love.

So, you see, well-meaning friends of all colors will take more than love to change this. Those of you who love me and mine—I see you. I appreciate you. And I love you back. Those of you who don't yet love me or just don't—you don't have to. But you can still co-create a world with me that reeks of justice instead of despair. And frankly, I'd rather have you pay attention to that.

Beloved, yes, let us love one another. But today, my siblings, understand we cannot wait on your love if it is limited to feeling warmly about us. Learn our racialized history. Learn about the road to eventual emancipation from slavery (yes—old history!) that was followed by a hundred years of legalized segregation (a newer history that we are barely 50 years removed from). Study the statistics that show that Black boys and girls are routinely and repeatedly disciplined and expelled from school far more frequently (for the same offenses) than white children. Read about how job applicants with "Black" names get far fewer callbacks than white applicants who have the same education and credentials. Arm yourself with love and knowledge, and let's work together for justice.

Almost ten years later, these are the words I have. Let's work together for justice.